Develop It Yourself

Develop It Yourself

SharePoint 2016

Out-Of-The-Box Features

By **D**inesh **G**autam

ISBN-13: 978-1540640901

ISBN-10: 1540640906

10 9 8 7 6 5 4 3 2 1

In loving memory

Dad

For my wife: Era!

"I can conquer the world with one hand,

as long as you're holding the other"

ABOUT THE AUTHOR

Dinesh Gautam (likes to be called just **Gautam**) has been a Principal SharePoint Consultant for many years. He has been working with SharePoint implementations, customization and administration since 2006. He strongly believes in the ideology of 80-20 rule i.e. providing solution minimum 80% based on SharePoint's out-of-the-box capabilities without writing any code and maximum 20% customization wherever required.

He stays with his wife in Mumbai, India and loves to travel. He is quite passionate about traveling on-site to work closely with clients and meeting people from various cultures.

He is a Microsoft Certified Solution Expert (MCSE) in SharePoint and is certified in SQL Server and .NET.

TABLE OF CONTENTS

INTRODUCTION

In today's world, "Centralization" is the key which has become the sure necessity, irrespective of the organization size, be it small or large.

SharePoint provides building blocks to create and manage integrated portals. It provides a collaborative platform for team members in the organization to work together to enhance productivity and that is the key to success.

Using Out-Of-The-Box features of SharePoint 2016 you can get some governance in place

- To demonstrate core collaborative features of SharePoint focusing on user productivity
- By looking at the differing features and understand what best fits the organization

I started my career in the late 90s as developer mainly on Microsoft platform. Those initial days of my career consist of ASP (legacy) pages, JavaScript files, and SQL server as a backend. That's all... But it really provided me an exposure to understand the web capability and power of centralization.

TARGET AUDIENCE

This book is intended for those readers, who are either already familiar with SharePoint or starting their career as a trainee to become SharePoint expert eventually... Nonetheless, this book should be a basic handbook for information workers and site managers to quickly build and manage content using SharePoint OOTB web parts.

GENERAL AUDIENCE

This book does not target IT professionals who are seeking in-depth knowledge about SharePoint 2016. Most of the topics have been touched upon to demonstrate the real supremacy of SharePoint out-of-the-box features.

THE TAKEAWAY FROM THIS BOOK

This book explores a lot of Out-of-The-Box (OOTB) features of SharePoint 2016 that would help you to understand the basic functionalities and deliver your solution either in no time or with a very little time/effort.

PRE-REQUISITES

To replicate the examples in this book, you should have following pre-requisites.

1. Access to at least one instance of SharePoint 2016 Test environment (On-premises / Online)
2. Adequate permission (ideally a contributor or administrator) for a site or site collection
3. Administrative rights to the server
4. A client computer running either Windows 7 or higher along with SharePoint Designer 2013.

BOOK STRUCTURE

Chapter 1: Out-of-The-Box Web Parts

This section describes all various groups of Web Parts that exist in SharePoint 2016. This section gives detailed information on how specific types of Web Parts can be configured to get the desired outcome.

Chapter 2: Out-of-The-Box Web Parts in Action

This section provides step-by-step, How-To, instructions to implement most widely used OOTB web parts in real-world scenarios. These web parts enable teams to present information on their sites to users in many different ways.

Chapter 3: SharePoint 2016 Search Capability

This section explores the uses of searching information within a local site collection and to search external sources to display the results along with local search results.

Chapter 4: SharePoint 2016 – Governance

This section provides an overview of content types along with managed metadata, term sets, and taxonomy. This section provides a high-level information needed to plan governance in their organization.

Chapter 5: SharePoint User Experience (UX)

This section provides the information on SharePoint navigation controls and quickly changing the look and feel of your site to enhance user experience.

Chapter 6: Extending Out-of-The-Box Functionality

This section introduces readers to creating custom forms and workflows for a list using Microsoft Designer 2013

CONVENTIONS

Develop It Yourself

It includes various exercises to implement few features at the end of each section. You can evaluate your knowledge gained and it will also help you to understand real-world scenarios along with proposed solution.

As you work through the exercises, you may find it difficult and need a hand-holding. But not to worry, to get step-by-step instructions for all the scenarios, you can visit our website.

Important	This icon marks something important to remember, such as, how you handle a particularly tricky part of SharePoint configuration.
Note	The note indicates key points and tips.
Settings	Additional settings that require configuration for SharePoint.
Example	Topics which are covered in details and explained in the example.
DIY	Develop It Yourself via exercises

ERRATA & BOOK SUPPORT

"To err is human", nonetheless I have put my best efforts to eliminate any typos or grammar mistakes. I've also made serious efforts to ensure the accuracy of this book. If you find an error in this book or want to suggest your two cents, I would really appreciate your feedback. Feel free to get in touch (email or website) should you require any additional support regarding the book or exercises mentioned in the book.

"WHAT & HOW"

Let's start with a vital question, what is SharePoint and how will it help you as an individual or an organization.

As Microsoft describes SharePoint as a business collaboration platform that makes it easier for people to work together.

On a high-level, SharePoint is a web-based software platform with a broad set of services that can speed up the development of web-based collaborative solutions and also offers the rich set of capabilities for creating real-world business solutions.

The goal of this book is to provide you a basic knowledge to use the tools and features of SharePoint. Each section in this book is defined in a way that enables you to develop no-code business solutions within SharePoint.

As an individual, you could be a developer or an information worker. In order to understand SharePoint's capabilities, in my opinion, you must define the goal to use SharePoint. As a developer, I will try to understand how to achieve a functionality whereas as a manager, I would be more focusing on what can be achieved through SharePoint.

From an organization perspective, the prime goal should be to focus on team collaboration, content management, social networking, searching the information and so on.

Microsoft grouped the features and services provided by SharePoint into five main categories of benefits:

1. Share
2. Organize
3. Discover
4. Build
5. Manage

Well, the whole idea of writing this book emerged with just one phrase "What and How". In this book, we will be covering the out-of-the-box web parts and few features in details to bypass theoretical definitions of SharePoint. It will not only save you some time but also give you an edge choosing the quick wins to wow your organization!!!

CHAPTER 1: OUT-OF-THE-BOX WEB PARTS

In this book, I will be focusing primarily on out-of-the-box web parts that are bundled with SharePoint 2016.

In general, Web Parts are essential components that can be used to develop sites and content quickly on web pages in SharePoint 2016. This way you can achieve most of the functionalities without any prior knowledge or technical background in SharePoint 2016.

Another good news is that once you configure any web part, you can export it and save it to Web Part Gallery with a unique name. This way it becomes fairly simple for you or others to reuse such pre-configured web parts in desired sites or/and pages.

Note

There are numerous Web Parts dependent on certain Features which need to be activated prior to using in site or pages. I will provide special comments for those Web Parts as we proceed further.

Next page onwards, there is a list of almost all Web Parts available in SharePoint 2016 with their respective categories.

APPS WEB PARTS

APPS Web part refers to various default or custom entities created for that site. These Web Parts display items from the List and Library apps created on your site. By default, you can add following contents to your page i.e.

1. Documents

When to use: To show the content of a specific library, starting in the root.

2. Form Templates

This library contains administrator-approved form templates that were activated to this site collection

When to use: Administrator-approved form templates are maintained in a special document library that can be accessed only by administrators.

3. Site Assets

Use this library to store files which are included on pages within this site, such as images on Wiki pages

When to use: You can use this folder to store site related objects like images, styles, etc. This is one of the best practices to store all your assets in a central repository.

4. Site Pages

When to use: There are two types of pages, WIKI and Web Part Pages

- WIKI page provides you an editor's version of the page to build and manage page content. You can use a wiki page to collaborate really effectively because it's easy to access information and share it with others within your team.

- A WEB PART Page contains various zones where you can only insert Web Parts from your SharePoint. However, you cannot add any content on the page directly using this web part.

5. Views

The App Web Parts allow you to add a view to your web pages. In most scenarios, you will be working with APP Web Part. Example: Employees is a custom list and will appear in Apps category.

When to use: You need to display list data in a tabular format with additional features like sorting, filter and search within the list data. In a real-world scenario, you can create a project dashboard to track project status and/or create connected web parts to display open tasks for a project.

Refer to screenshot below

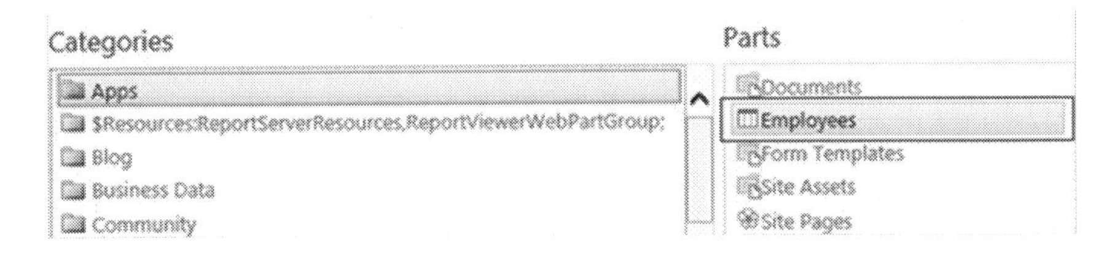

Figure 1.1 APPS Web Part

Example

You can see "Views" web parts in action in our upcoming chapter where we will explore in details. Stay connected...

BLOG WEB PARTS

As per Microsoft definition, a blog is a Web site that enables you or your organization to share ideas and information quickly. Blogs contain posts that are dated and listed in reverse chronological order. People can comment on your posts as well as provide links to interesting sites, photos, and related blogs.

Blog posts can be created quickly and they often have an informal tone or provide a unique perspective. Although blogs are frequently used for commentary on the Internet, they can be used in several ways in a corporate environment.

When to use: As a manager, you can use the blog post to make an announcement or provide info on new policies, team members can share their knowledge about their projects, or technicians can publish the how-to material guide.

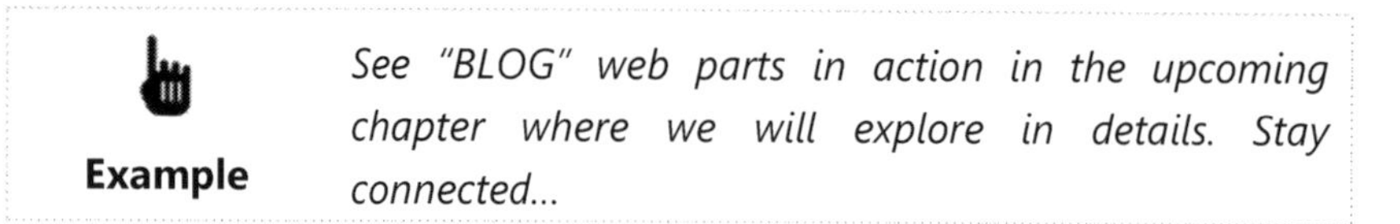

Example *See "BLOG" web parts in action in the upcoming chapter where we will explore in details. Stay connected...*

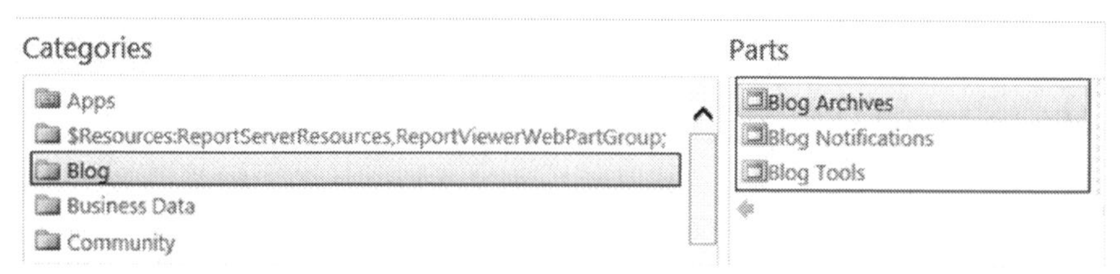

Figure 1.2 BLOG Web Part

BLOG Web Part

Blog provides web parts functionality for a blog site

1. Blog Archives

Provides quick links to older blog posts

Blog Archives

Archives

August

OLDER POSTS

Figure 1.3 Blog Archives

2. Blog Notifications

Provides quick links to register for blog posts notifications using Alerts or RSS feed

3. Blog Tools

Provides blog owners and administrators with quick links to common settings pages and content lists for managing a blog site.

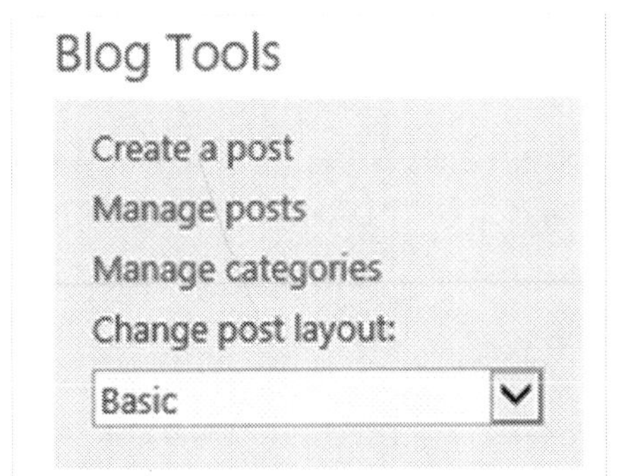

Figure 1.4 Blog Tools

BUSINESS DATA WEB PARTS

The Business Data Web Parts are designed to work with data from an external list. An external list is another useful functionality of SharePoint to fetch data from various line of business (LOB) systems using Business Connectivity Services (BCS).

These Business Data Web Parts help you to display additional information for status and indicators. These web parts provide a functionality to connect to Excel workbook as a page and enable users to view Visio web drawings as well.

When to use: You have an external application "Leave Management" and want to display leave details on SharePoint page. You wish to get info for reimbursement or purchase requests that are stored in other LOB application.

Note

The scope of creating External List (BCS) is out of scope for this book as it would require a basic understanding of SharePoint environment, SharePoint Designer, and other configurations.

Business Data group provides web parts functionality for retrieving data from the external system and making it available within SharePoint site.

1. Business Data Actions

Displays a list of items from an external list (Business Data Connectivity).

2. Business Data Connectivity Filter

Filters the contents of a connected Business Data Web Part by using a list of values from an external list.

3. Business Data Item

Displays an item from an external list.

4. Business Data Item Builder

Creates a Business Data item from parameters in a URL query string and provides it to other Business Data Web Parts.

5. Business Data List

Displays a list of items from an external list.

6. Business Data Related List

Displays a list of child items related to a parent item from an external list. Requires an association.

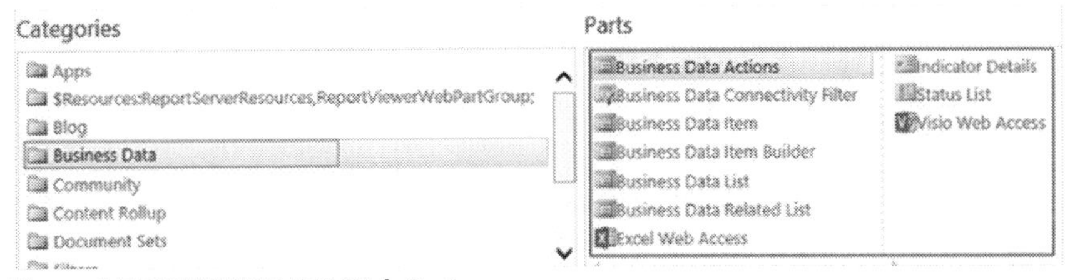

Figure 1.5 BUSINESS DATA Web Parts

COMMUNITY WEB PARTS

Community-related web parts enable users to display Community description, join the community, display membership information, administration tools and statistics within a community site.

When to use: Communities are the best way to engage your team through discussions. You can define separate categories to organize discussions. You can encourage your team to view and contribute to the discussions on a regular basis. For example, you can post a question on a forum about New Year bash theme and get interesting replies.

Important

You can integrate these community features on team sites, records sites, project sites, and so on.

Note

The scope of using Community web parts is out of scope for this book as it would require a basic understanding of SharePoint environment, SharePoint Designer, and other configurations.

Community group web parts features are as follows

1. About this community

This web part displays the community description and other properties like established date. This web part will work on Community sites or any other site that has Community Features turned on.

2. Join

Provides the ability for non-members of a community site to join the community. The button hides itself if the user is already a member. This web part will work on Community sites or any other site that has Community Features turned on.

3. My membership

Displays an item from an external list.

4. Business Data Item Builder

Displays reputation and membership information for the current visitor of a community site. This web part will work on Community sites or any other site that has Community Features turned on.

5. Tools

Provides community owners and administrators with quick links to common settings pages and content lists for managing a community site. This web part will work on Community sites or any other site that has Community Features turned on.

6. What's happening

Displays the number of members, topics and replies within a community site. This web part will work on Community sites or any other site that has Community Features turned on.

Figure 1.6 COMMUNITY Web Parts

CONTENT ROLLUP WEB PARTS

As it is self-explanatory, these web parts allow you to roll up content regardless of actual location. You can use these web parts to rolling up search results, provide project summaries, display timelines and fetch relevant documents across the sites.

When to use: You have various different project sites with respective tasks and subtasks. You need to display Project status report i.e. tasks which are not 100% completed. This will help you to track project(s) easily and act accordingly with your mitigation plan in hand.

Note

In chapter 2, we will be focusing primarily on web parts from this group. In a real-world scenario, you will find widely used web parts namely Content Query, Content Search, RSS Feed, etc.

Content Rollup group web parts features are as follows

1. Categories

Displays categories from the Site Directory.

2. Content Query

Displays a dynamic view of content from your site.

Example

See "Content Query" web part in the action in our upcoming chapter where we will explore in details.

Stay connected...

3. Content Search

Content Search Web Part will allow you to show items that are results of a search query you specify.
When you add it to the page, this Web Part will show recently modified items from the current site. You can change this setting to show items from another site or list by editing the Web Part and changing its search criteria. As new content is discovered by search, this Web Part will display an updated list of items each time the page is viewed.

Example

See Content Search Web Part in action in our upcoming chapter where we will explore in details. Stay connected...

4. Project Summary

Displays information about a project in an easy to read overview.

5. Relevant Documents

Displays documents that are relevant to the current user.

6. RSS Viewer

Displays an RSS feed.

Example

See "RSS Viewer" web part in the action in our upcoming chapter where we will explore in details. Stay connected...

7. Site Aggregator

Displays sites of your choice.

8. Sites in Category

Displays sites from the Site Directory within a specific category

9. Term Property

Displays the specified property of a Term

10. Timeline

Use this timeline to show a high level view of data from another web part or tasks list

11. WSRP Viewer

Displays portlets from web sites using WSRP 1.1

12. XML Viewer

Transforms XML data using XSL and shows the results

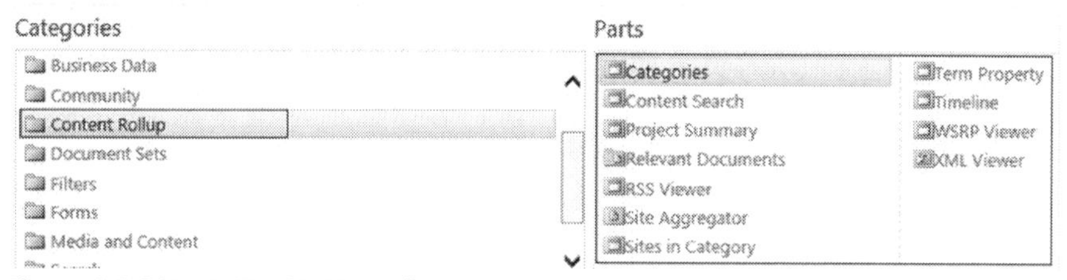

Figure 1.7 CONTENT ROLLUP Web Parts

DOCUMENT SETS WEB PARTS

A Document Set is a group of related documents that you can manage as a single entity.

In simpler words, it can be defined as a content type. You have a choice of using out-of-the-box content types or create a new custom content type.

You have full control of its characteristics and metadata. It also helps in organizing multiple office documents in a single entity such as Word documents, OneNote notebooks, PowerPoint presentations, Visio diagrams, excel workbooks, etc.

When to use: You are an Insurance company with various products (general, health, etc.) that need to be stored in SharePoint. Each product contains different metadata, digital assets, etc. You can create different templates based on your requirement and attach metadata to the products. This improves the Search results and every visitor gets all the details of insurance plans. The document set is a great way of managing literature and content where a common need exists, such as a claim, business case or RFP.

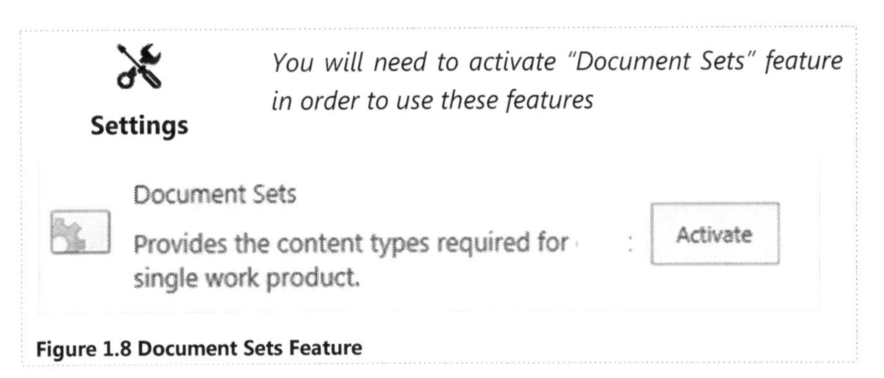

Figure 1.8 Document Sets Feature

Note

The scope of using Document Sets web parts is out of scope for this book as it would require basic understanding of SharePoint environment, SharePoint Designer, and other configurations

Document Sets group web parts features are as follows

1. Document Set Contents

Displays the contents of the Document Set.

2. Document Set Properties

Displays the properties of the Document Set.

Figure 1.9 DOCUMENT SET Web Parts

FILTERS WEB PARTS

Filters Web Parts provide various options to limit the results based on provided value(s). Generally, users can use manual filters or automatic filters. Manual filters are those where users provide the values which are applied to List View Web Parts. In the case of automatic filters, it applies the filters without user's involvement (for example, manual activities such as input keyword followed by button click).

Automatic Web Part Filters could be used to filter the values by- current logged-in user, specific date and text values set by the user. You can also use query string (URL) parameter to filter List View Web Part for e.g. *CustomPage.aspx?filter=yourValue*

Manual Web part Filters could be used to filter the values by- Text Filter, Date Filter, etc. Once user inputs or selects values then these filters are applied on the page to display filtered results.

When to use: You need to view all the tasks which have been assigned to you. You need to search projects based on status or date range.

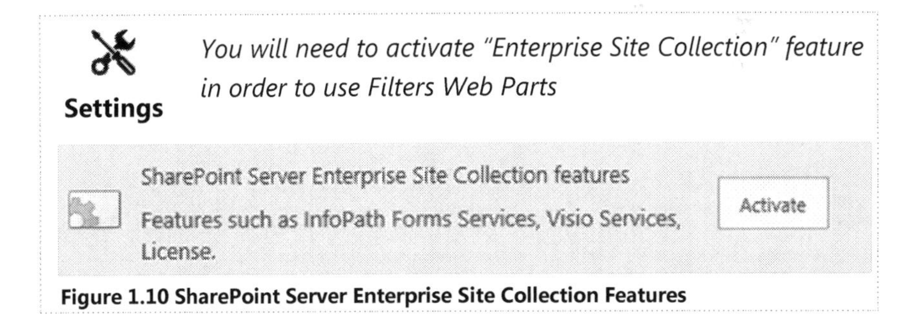

Figure 1.10 SharePoint Server Enterprise Site Collection Features

Filters Web Parts at a glance

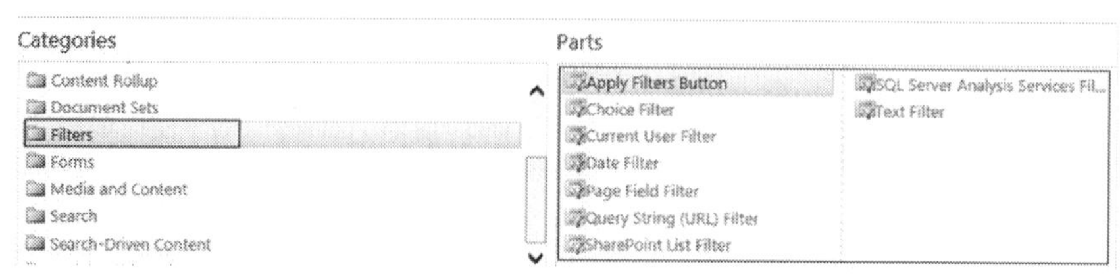

Figure 1.11 Filters Web Part

FILTERS Web Parts

1. Apply Filters Button

Add this button to a page so users can decide when to apply their filter choices. Otherwise, each filter is applied when its value is changed.

2. Choice Filter

Filters the contents of Web Parts using a list of values entered by the page author.

Figure 1.12 Department Filter

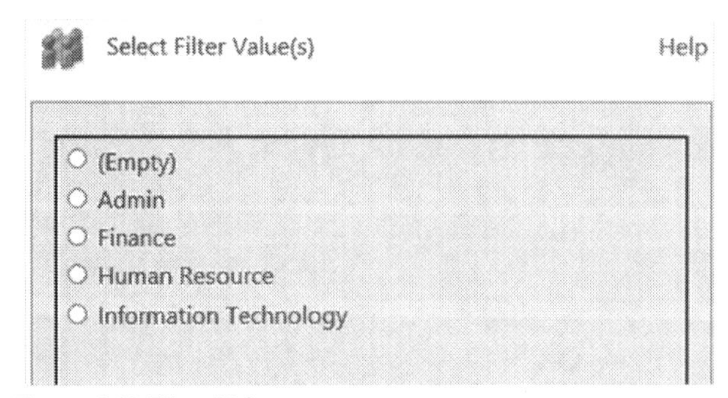

Figure 1.13 Filter Values

3. Current User Filter

Filters the contents of Web Parts by using properties of the current user.

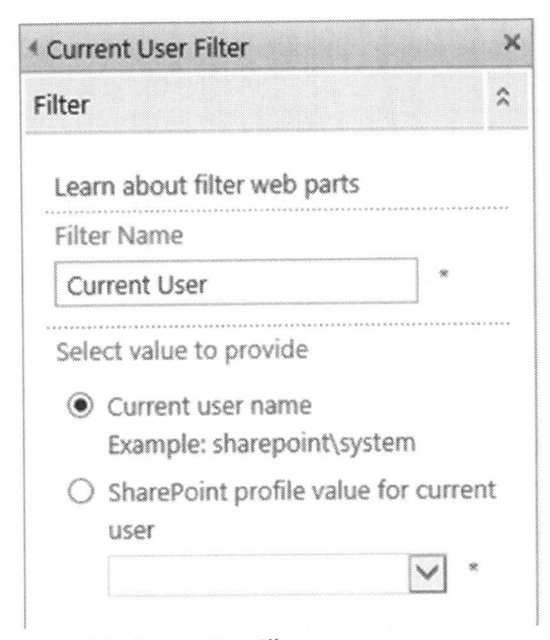

Figure 1.14 Current User Filter

Note

In order to use "SharePoint profile value for current user", it will require creation and configuration of "User Profile Service", otherwise the drop down list will be empty and the user will not be able to select any value.

4. Date Filter

Filter the contents of Web Parts by allowing users to enter or pick a date.

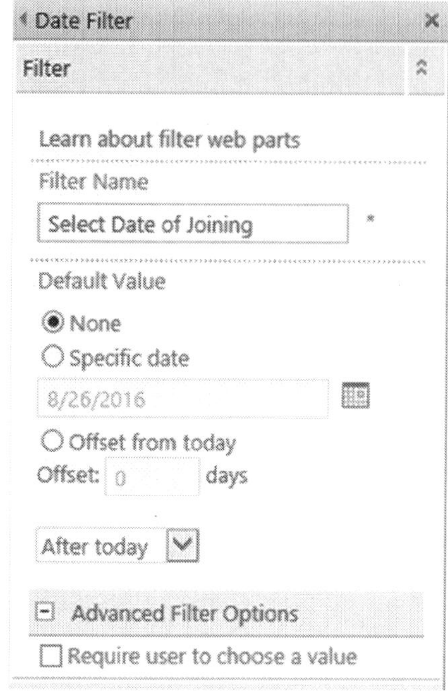

Figure 1.15 Date Filter

Filter Name: Filter Web Part name

Default Value:

- ***None:*** no condition
- ***Specific date:*** user can provide any pre-selected date
- ***Offset from Today***

  Offset: number of days (numeric)

After / Before Today: User can define offset days before or after from today

Advanced Filter Options

- ***Require user to choose a value:*** *User can leave it unchecked (clear) if date filter is optional. You need to mark (select) it if the date is compulsory to apply the filter based on selected date.*

Figure 1.16 Date Filter

5. Page Field Filter

Filters the contents of Web Parts using information about the current page.

Using this filter, you can use any one of the values (Title, Created or Modified) to filter one or more web parts on the current page.

Figure 1.17 Page Field Filter

You can also use advanced options to handle multiple values via sending single value, all values or combining into a single value.

The associated web part will filter the results, based on the values provided by this filter.

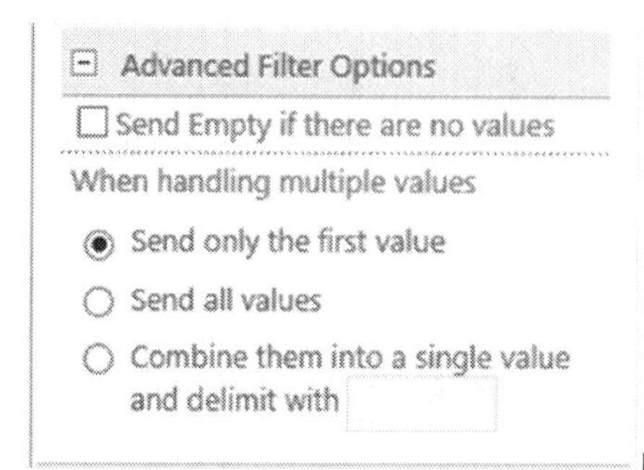

Figure 1.18 Advanced Filter Options

6. Query String (URL) Filter

Filters the contents of Web Parts using values passed via the query string.

Using Filter Web Part, you can define a parameter and append it to query string for further use. It will enable automatic filtering on other Web Parts based on query string parameter.

For example, you can create a Web Part Page having employee details working in the organization. Each employee belongs to a different department (Admin, Human Resource, Finance, etc.), you can create separate links for each department. Once the user clicks on these links, it will show records pertaining to that specific department.

Admin

http://mycompany.sharepoint.com/pages/Dept.aspx?dept=Admin

Human Resource

http://mycompany.sharepoint.com/pages/Dept.aspx?dept=Human%20Resource

Finance

http://mycompany.sharepoint.com/pages/Dept.aspx?dept=Finance

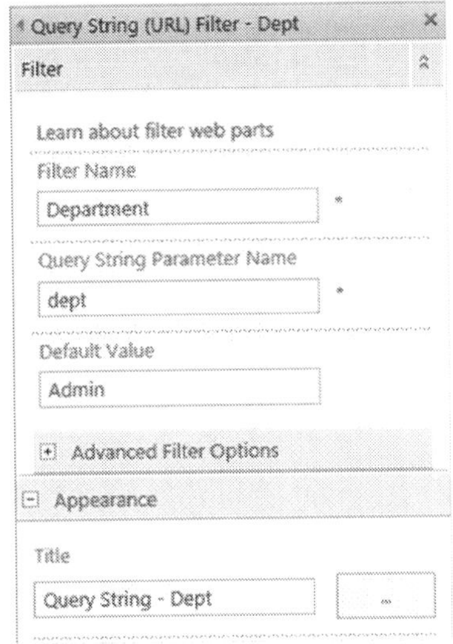

Figure 1.19 Query String Filter

7. SharePoint List Filter

Filters the contents of Web Parts by using a list of values.

Using List Filter Web Part, you can provide filter values directly from another list. These values would be populated as a list of choices and you do not need to provide any values manually. You can choose list column from selected list and also provides an option to differentiate the value used for filter and display it to the user on the page.

For example, you can pass Employee ID to filter another list web part whereas Title field can be used for a display purpose i.e. to select values from list filter.

!

Important

In order to view all available columns, you need to select "Full list view" from View section.

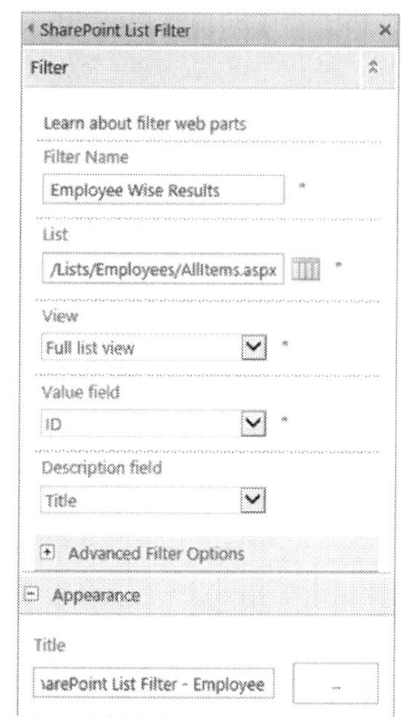

Figure 1.20 List Filter

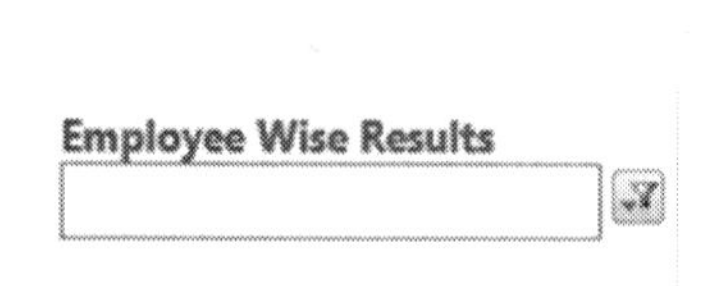

Figure 1.21 Employee Filter

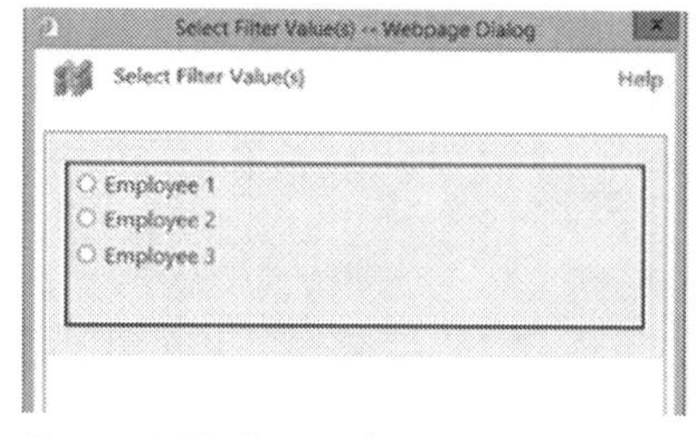

Figure 1.22 Filter Values

8. SQL Server Analysis Services Filter

Filters the contents of Web Parts using a list of values from SQL Server Analysis Services cubes.

! **Important**	*It requires SSAS Cube (Office Data Connection file) to send filter information to another web part.*

Note

The scope of creating and configuring Cube is out of scope for this book as this is an advanced topic which would require an in-depth understanding of writing MDX queries to create Cube.

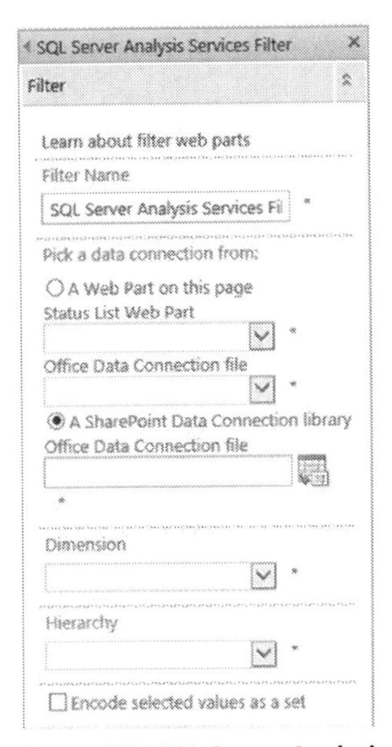

Figure 1.23 SQL Server Analysis Services Filter

9. Text Filter

Filters the contents of Web Parts by allowing users to enter a text value.

Text Filter Web Part allows users to send typed values to another web part. You need to include this web part along with list/Library web part to filter results.

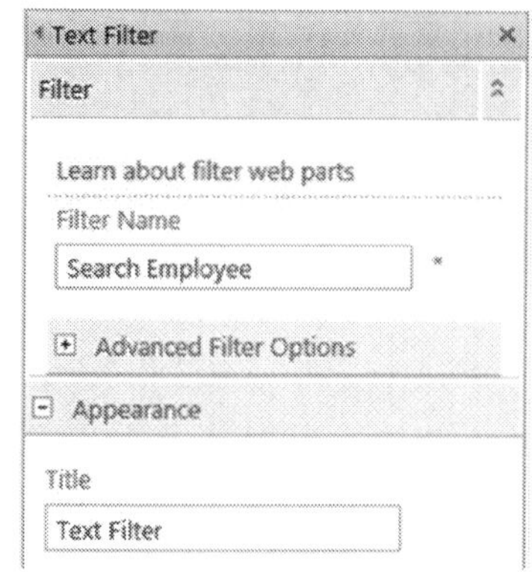

Figure 1.24 Text Filter

Next, you need to create web part connections between these two web parts in order to send values to source web part.

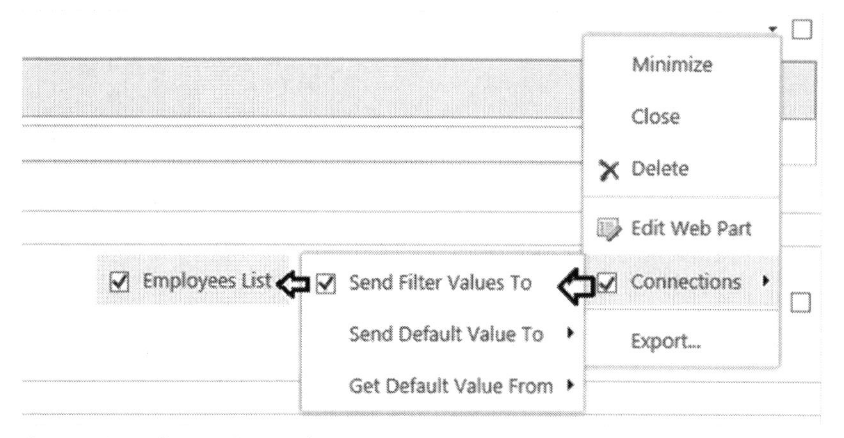

Figure 1.25 Web Part Connection

A pop-up window will be shown to set the connection attributes.

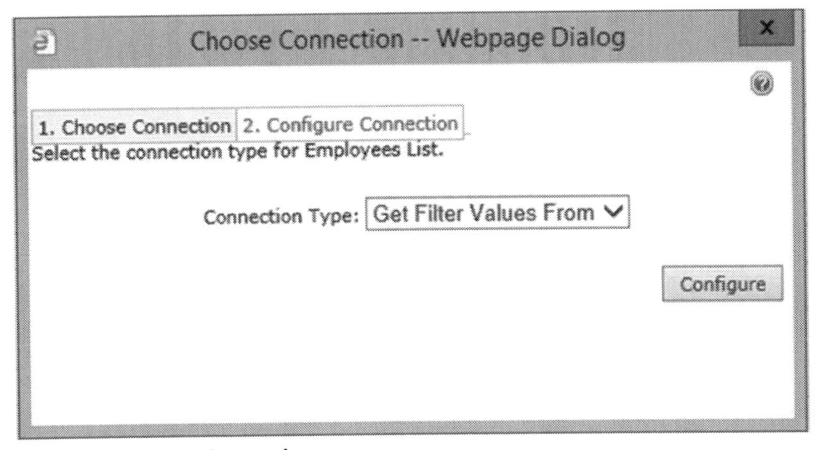

Figure 1.26 Choose Connection

Configure Connection -- Webpage Dialog

1. Choose Connection 2. Configure Connection

Connection Settings

Provider Field Name **Search Employee**

Consumer Field Name Title

Finish Cancel

Figure 1.27 Configure Connection

Once web part connection has been created then the user can type a keyword to search in employee title field.

Figure 1.28 Search Employee

This value will search in one of the specified columns for that list. Though there are multiple limitations to this approach i.e.

1. User can search values only in one of the column

2. The search is based on exact keyword and doesn't search partial keywords. For e.g. If Title of Employee list is "Employee 1" then the user needs to search for "Employee 1" and "Employee" will not return any value.

However, the good news is that SharePoint 2016 (SharePoint 2013 onwards) consists of a new feature where the user can enable "Show Search box" within the list web part.

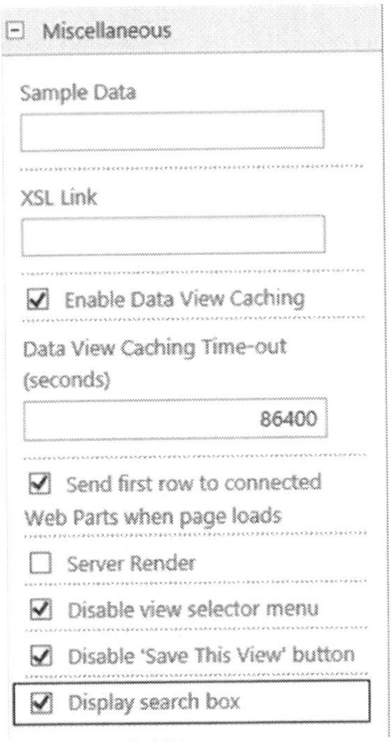

Miscellaneous
Sample Data
XSL Link
Enable Data View Caching
Data View Caching Time-out (seconds)
86400
Send first row to connected Web Parts when page loads
Server Render
Disable view selector menu
Disable 'Save This View' button
Display search box

Figure 1.29 Miscellaneous Section

This feature allows the user to search keyword in Searchable columns. Well, I leave it to you, to decide which option is more suitable for your requirements.

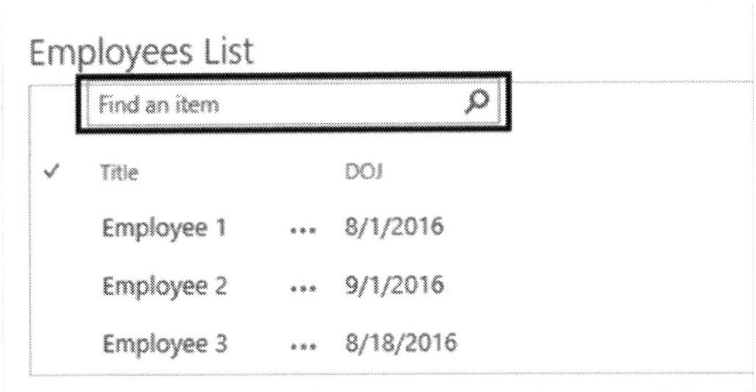

Employees List
Find an item

Title	DOJ
Employee 1	8/1/2016
Employee 2	9/1/2016
Employee 3	8/18/2016

Figure 1.30 Employee List

FORMS WEB PARTS

This category consists of two web parts namely, HTML Form and InfoPath Form.

Using HTML Form Web Part, you can write/embed custom HTML code to create a form. This web part provides a single text box along with a button to start with. Using your custom HTML code, you can render HTML controls and can also be connected to other web parts on a page.

InfoPath Form Web Part allows you to embed an InfoPath form on a page. But first, you need to create an InfoPath form in a form library. This is a good option to display InfoPath form within the browser itself.

Note

The scope of using Form Web Parts are out of scope for this book as it would require a basic understanding of SharePoint environment, SharePoint Designer, and other configurations.

!

Important

InfoPath Status for SharePoint 2016

SharePoint 2016 on premise does support InfoPath browser forms (contrary to earlier statements).

Office 365 will support InfoPath browser forms in SharePoint Online 'until further notice' officially, with indications that may mean until one year after the release of Office 2016.

InfoPath browser forms with code do not work on SharePoint Online InfoPath browser forms do not work on mobile devices when SharePoint Online mobile view is enabled.

There are reports of problems using InfoPath 2013 with Outlook 2016 email.

Reference:

http://www.formotus.com/16643/blog-infopath/microsoft-announces-future-infopath

Forms group web parts features are as follows

1. HTML Form Web Part

Connects simple form controls to other Web Parts.

When to use: you can use HTML Form Web Part to select a department from the drop-down list, pass the value to a List View Web Part of employee data, and filter the data by that department.

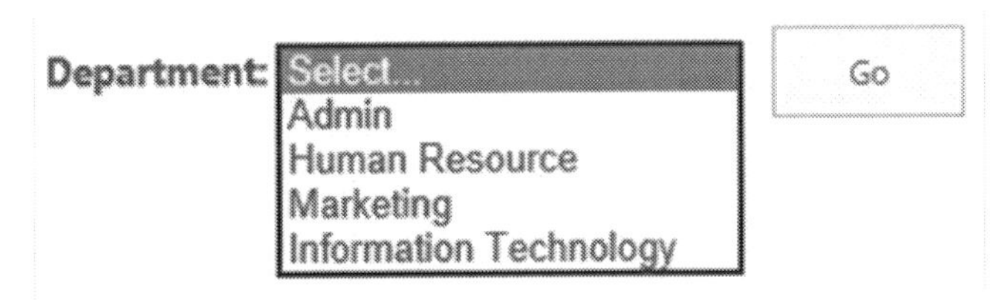

Figure 1.31 HTML Form Web Part

2. InfoPath Form Web Part

Use this Web Part to display an InfoPath browser-enabled form.

When to use:

If you want to manage your Customers and Orders list data on the same page. On viewing or editing items in a Customers list, you can also manage all Orders for that customer from the related Orders list.

When filing out a new customer requirement form, you can automatically fill in the contact information by using data from the Customers list by selecting an item in the Customers list Web Part and sending the values into the fields in the requirement form in the InfoPath Form Web Part.

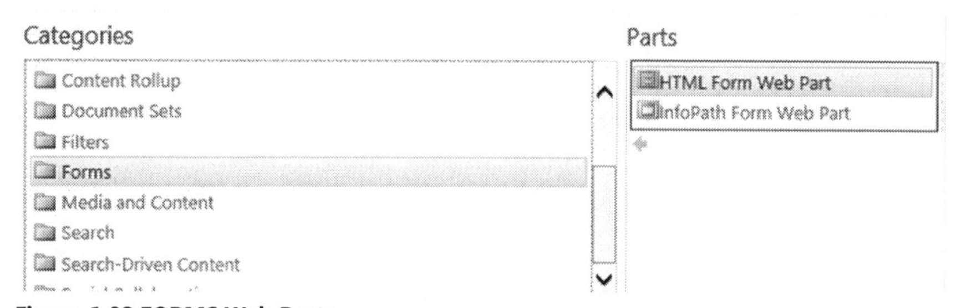

Figure 1.32 FORMS Web Parts

MEDIA AND CONTENT

As the name suggests, this category provides a myriad of web parts to work with. It provides an array of web parts that could be used in defining layout and design of the page, create custom content or more importantly embed your JavaScript code snippets.

This group provides media related web parts to use audio, video or image files on a page. You can choose to run the Silverlight application, to provide a rich interactive experience to end users.

Using Content Editor Web Part, you can quickly render HTML output without any prior experience. With a little effort, you can insert custom styles to make it more presentable.

If you wish to replicate this functionality in multiple pages or sites then all you need to do is to export this Web Part to SharePoint gallery. This way you can reuse this web part across pages or sites.

Media and Content group web parts features are as follows

1. Content Editor

Allows authors to enter rich text content.

Content Editor Web Part provides a very user-friendly way to input text, media files, styles or custom code. It doesn't require any prior technical knowledge unless you want to play around with JavaScript. Content contributors will find it very handy to populate contents on the fly without any much effort.

When to use: You can make your SharePoint page more visually appealing and add emphasis, by utilizing headings, images, and explanatory content. As shown in next image, the final layout was created using a table, well-formatted paragraph, and image. You can also create a set of hyperlinks that link to additional information.

Good News!!!

SharePoint 2016 is released

Figure 1.33 CONTENT EDITOR Web Part

2. Get started with your site

This web part displays a set of tiles with common SharePoint actions.

"Get started with your site" Web part provides quick access links (shortcuts) to get you started with the site. This web part is included by default on a home page post site creation. There are many quick links which in turn helps you to organize, connect, share and personalize your look and feel.

Settings

You will need to activate "Getting Started" feature in order to use this Web Parts.

Figure 1.34 Getting Started Feature

Get Started with your site web part displays various tiles as mentioned below

Title	Description
Share Your Site	**Connect** - It helps you to share your site with other users. You can also achieve the same functionality using "Share" button located at the top ribbon.
Working on a deadline?	**Organize** - It helps you to get organized via task status, deadline, and upcoming calendar events. You can quickly create tasks and calendar entries.
Add lists, libraries, and other apps	**Manage Content** – It allows you to add a new APP i.e. Document Library, Custom List, etc.
What's your style	**Design and Layout** - It allows you to pick your favorite style from preloaded templates, based on your preferences. If you have adequate rights then you can change it via site settings configuration as well.
Your site. Your brand	**Branding** - You can quickly set the Title for your site along with a description. You can also replace the default logo with your Company Logo.

Figure 1.35 Get Started With Your Site (On-Premises)

Get started with your site - On Premises

➢ **Keep email in context** (O365 Only)

Integration - You can share email on your site and connect documents to Outlook. It would help you to be in sync with your documents, email, and calendars in Outlook and SharePoint.

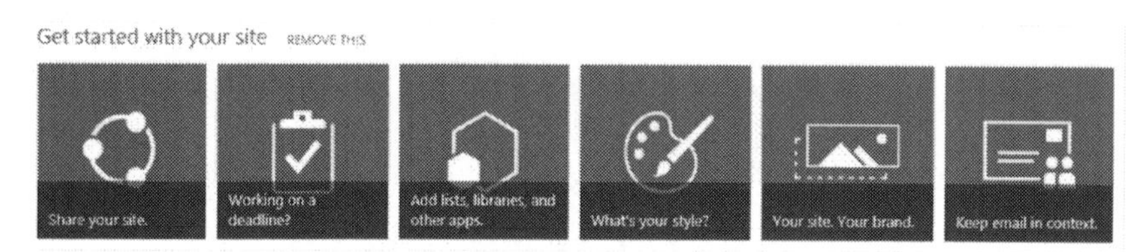

Figure 1.36 Get Started With Your Site (O365)

Get started with your site - O365

3. Image Viewer

Displays a specified image.

If you wish to show an image on a page then you can do it quickly with Image Viewer Web Part. It allows you to insert image or other graphics to a web part page or use the image directly on the wiki page.

You can configure its properties such as dimensions (Height, Width), alignment (Vertical, horizontal). You also have a choice to keep it transparent or with the custom background color.

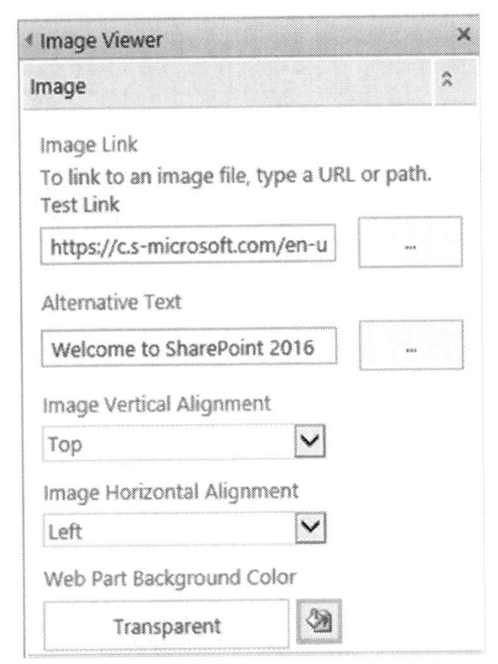

Figure 1.37 IMAGE VIEWER Web Part - Settings

Once you are done with configuring the settings, it would be displayed on the page as shown below.

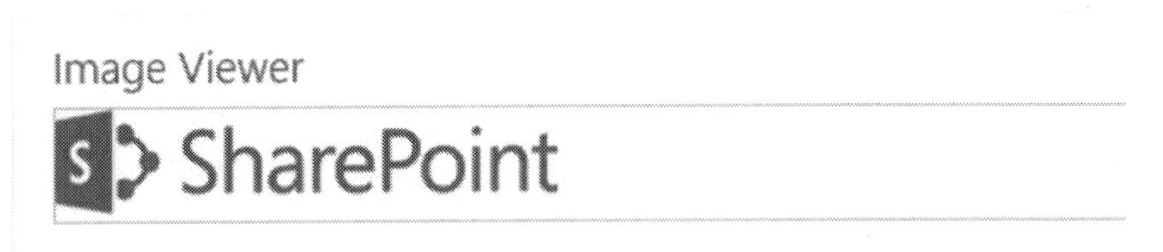

Figure 1.38 IMAGE VIEWER Web Part –Final Output

4. Media Web Part

Use to embed media clips (video and audio) in a web page.

Media Web Part lets you add an audio or video on your page. You have multiple options to add media i.e. computer, SharePoint or direct media link. This web part provides you to show a thumbnail image for the video. You can configure media properties to start media automatically, loop until stopped and lock Aspect ratio. You can also set horizontal and vertical size for the media.

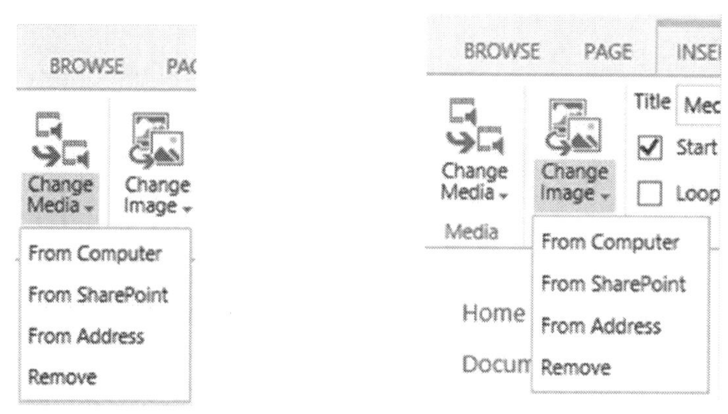

Figure 1.39 Media Options **Figure 1.40 Image Options**

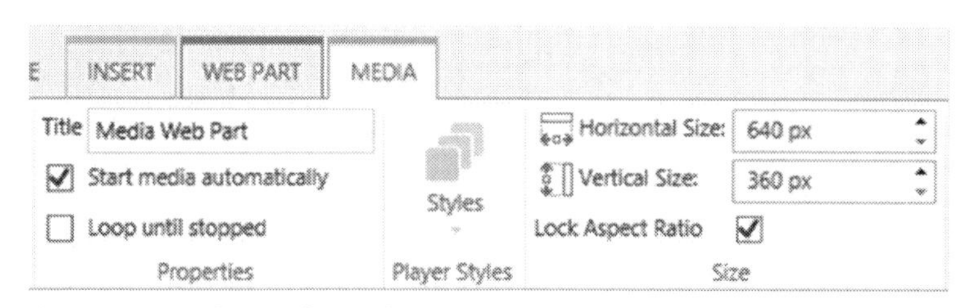

Figure 1.41 Media Configuration

Media Web Part supports specific formats as mentioned below

- HTML5 - asf, avi, mpg, mp3, mp4, ogg, ogv, webm, wma, wmv
- Classic Silverlight Media Web Part - asf, mp3, mp4, wma, wmv

Figure 1.42 MEDIA Web Part

5. Page Viewer

Displays another Web page on this Web page. The other Web page is presented in an iframe.

Page Viewer Web Part allows you to embed a web page, folder or file on a page. The content is displayed within an iframe, you can simply imagine it like a small window within your page.

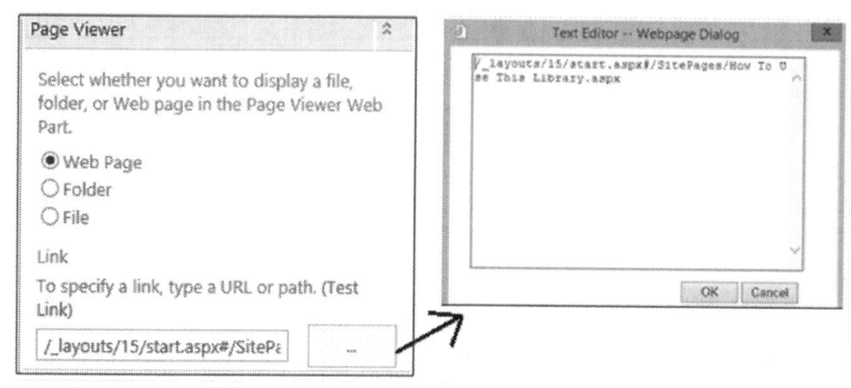

Figure 1.43 PAGE VIEWER Web Part – Settings

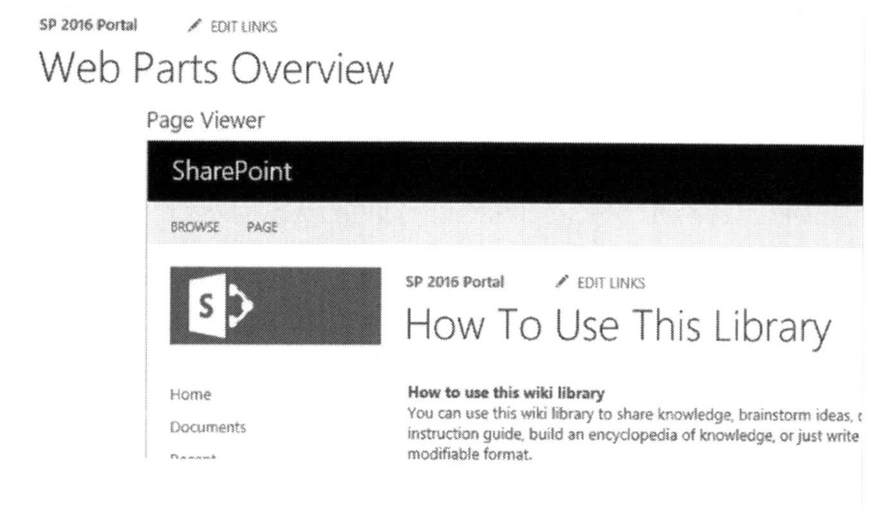

Figure 1.44 Page Viewer Iframe

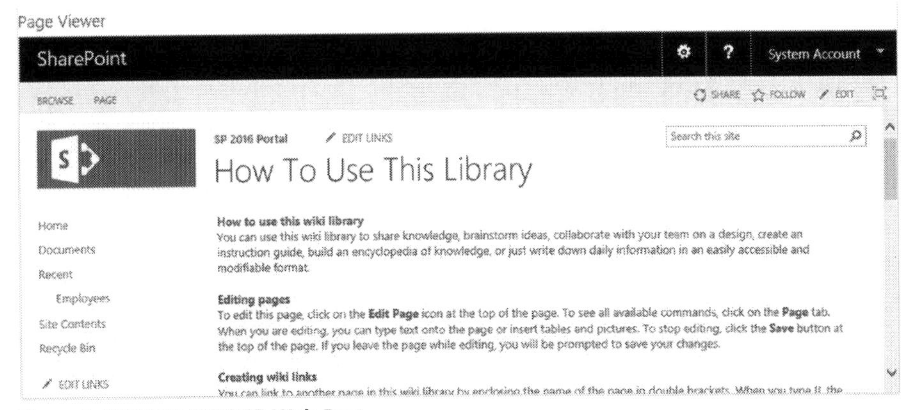

Figure 1.45 PAGE VIEWER Web Part

6. Picture Library Slideshow Web Part

Use to display a slideshow of images and photos from a picture library.

Picture Library Slideshow Web Part provides you for selecting existing picture library in order to create a slide show. You need to create an app of type "Picture Library" and upload images to this picture library.

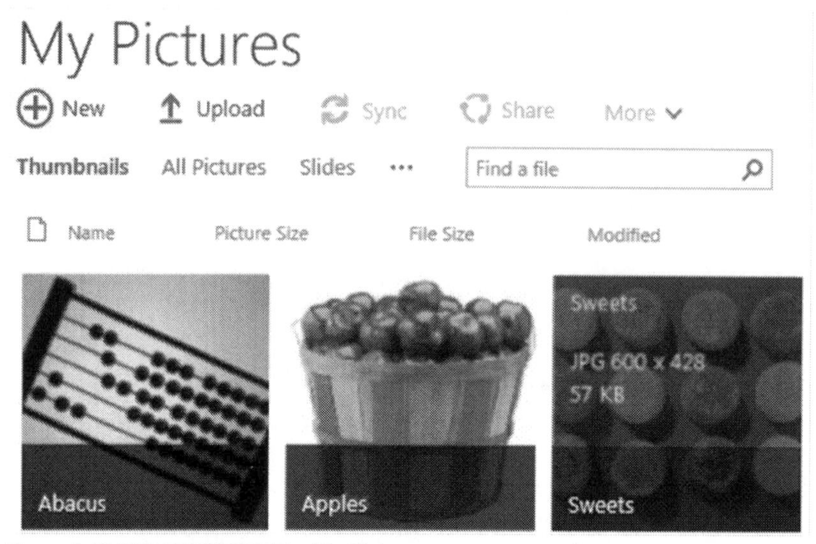

Figure 1.46 PICTURE LIBRARY – My Pictures

Once you add Slideshow web part to your page, it will show all picture libraries in its Picture Library drop down list. You can select your desired picture library, which you wish to create slideshow from. You can define Duration to Show Picture (seconds), display order (sequential or random) and Library view (All Pictures, Thumbnails or Slide).

You can configure property, either to show toolbar or hide it. This web part could be further configured to include other fields like Title, Description along with its position (beside or below image)

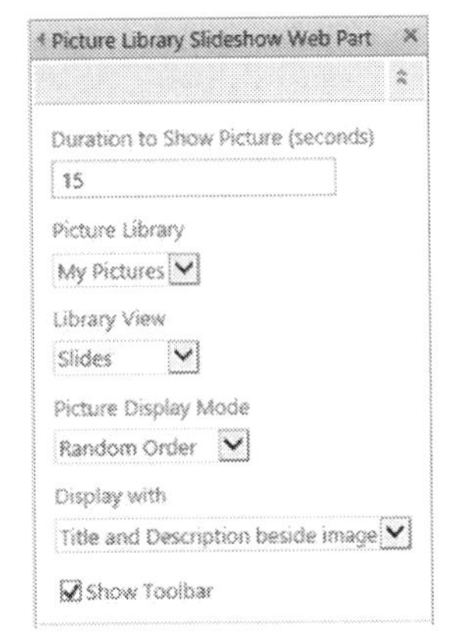

Figure 1.47 Settings

Figure 1.48 Picture Library Slideshow in action

7. Script Editor

Allows authors to insert HTML snippets or scripts.

8. Silverlight Web Part

A web part to display a Silverlight application.

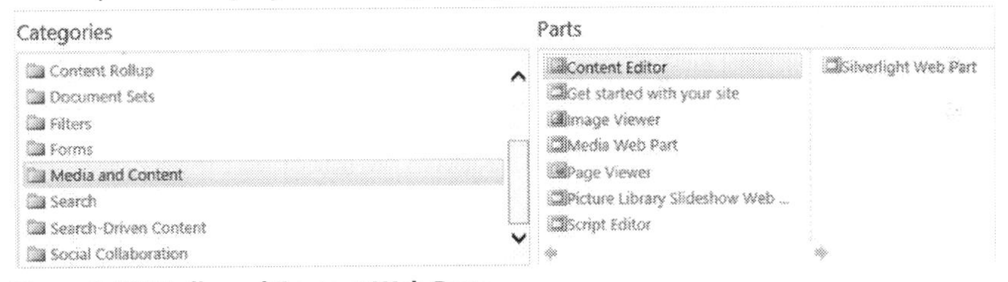

Figure 1.49 Media and Content Web Parts

SEARCH

Though this topic is intended for advanced users but I will try to provide a high-level overview that should help you to understand the core functionality of these web parts in order to make the most use of it.

There are scenarios where you might get confused whether to use Content Query Web Part or Content Search Web Part. For this book, that comparison is out of context and I will concentrate only on exact details required pertaining to this section.

Search category provides a set of web parts which help users to create refiners, search results, navigation based on metadata and of course with the help of search box, the user can filter data on specific search results.

Search group web parts features are as follows

1. Refinement

This web part helps the users to refine search results

Using this web part, you can narrow down the search results into categories that would help to get relevant data.

As an admin, you can apply refiners to get specific data from various Search Results Web Part.

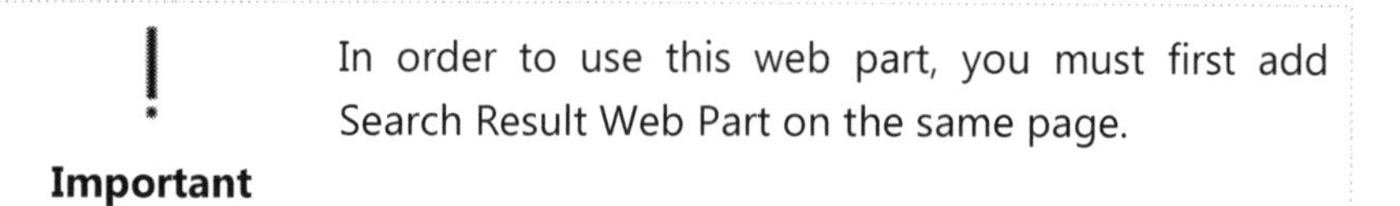

Important

In order to use this web part, you must first add Search Result Web Part on the same page.

Note

As mentioned earlier, this is an advanced topic and few pre-requisites need to be completed prior to using this web part. We need to set managed properties to be used as refiners that must be set to ***Refinable*** and ***Queryable*** in the search schema.

For example, you can add "Department" refinement to Search Result Web Part. This way you can narrow down the search to get Department wise data.

There are additional settings that we can change as well such as

- Specify which refiners to show.
- Change the display template for a refiner.
- Change display names for refiners.
- Add counts to refiners.

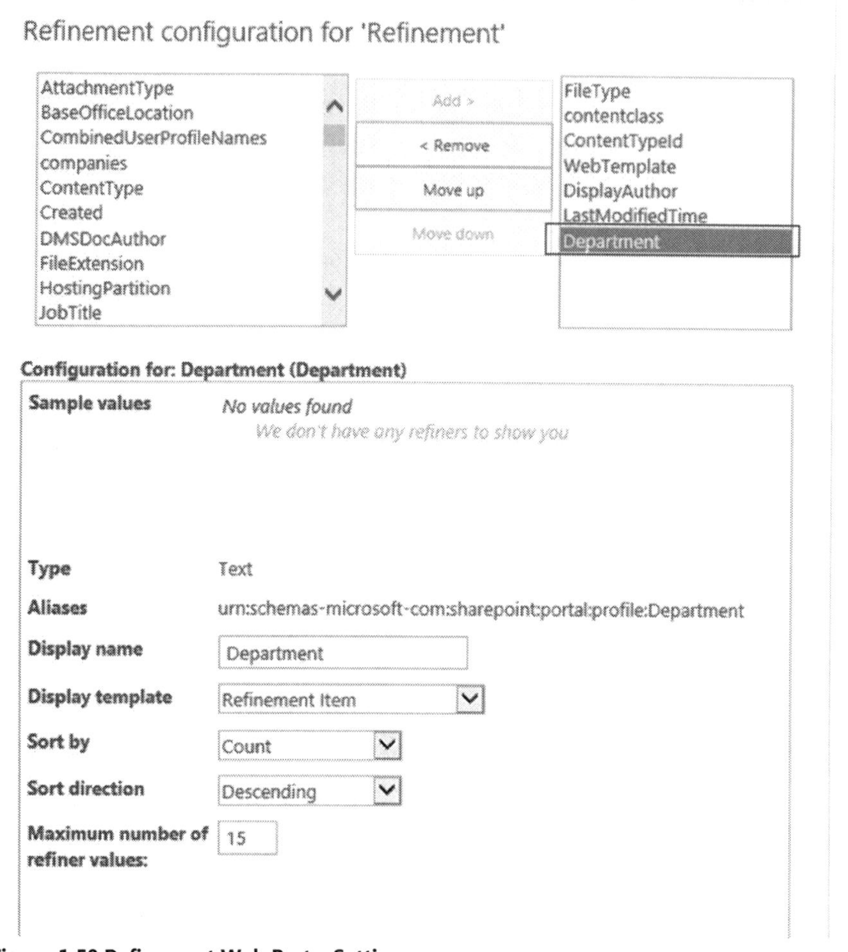

Figure 1.50 Refinement Web Part – Settings

2. Search Box

Displays a search box that allows users to search for information.

Using Search Box Web Part, you can configure it to pass the value to other Search Results Web Part on the same page.

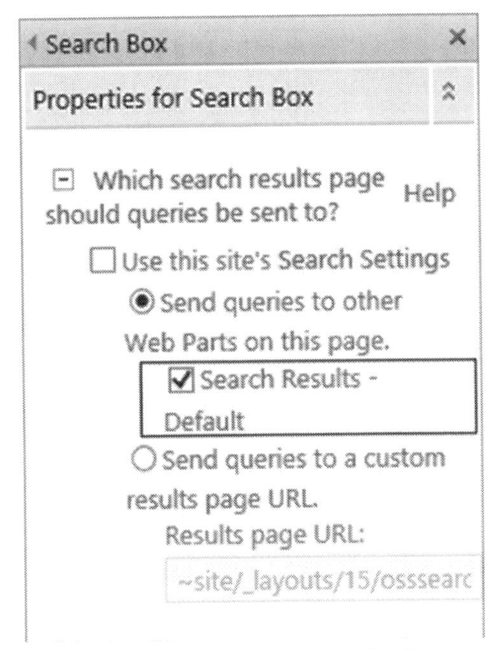

Figure 1.51 Refinement Web Part – Settings

Going forward, once the user enters any keyword and clicks search button then connected Search Result Web Part will be filtered accordingly.

Figure 1.52 Search Box Textbox

3. Search Navigation

This web part helps the users to navigate among search verticals

By default, there are default verticals (scope) available in any search center

1. Everything
2. People
3. Conversations
4. Video
5. This Site

Before using the Search Navigation Web Part, you need to first add new vertical.

In order to add new vertical,

1. Go to site settings and select search settings under Search section
2. In section Configure Search Navigation, add a new scope.

For example, you can add "google"

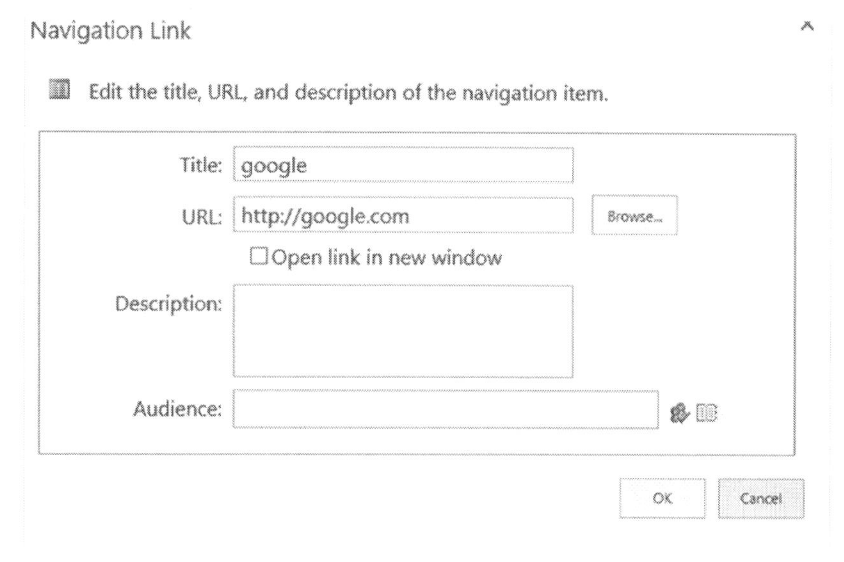

Figure 1.53 Navigation Link

3. Click OK to save the changes

Note Apart from Search Center, you need to add all other verticals. These are already added by default in Search Center ONLY.

You can create those verticals using the following table.

Everything	{search-center}/Pages/results.aspx
People	{search-center}/Pages/peopleresults.aspx
Conversations	{search-center}/Pages/ Conversationresults.aspx
Videos	{search-center}/Pages/ videoresults.aspx

After adding above verticals (as per your requirement), it will look as shown below.

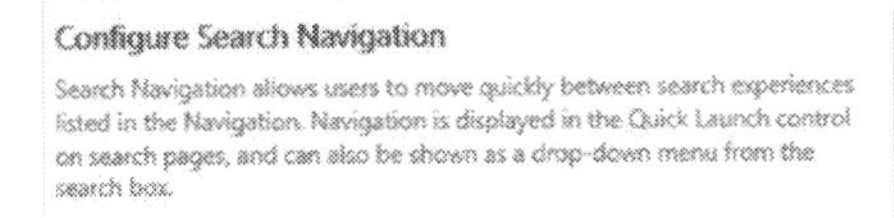

Figure 1.54 Configure Search Navigation

Once you have set those verticals properly then it would reflect in Search Navigation Web Part.

Perry

everything people coversations google

Figure 1.55 Custom Refinement

4. Search Results

Displays the search results and the properties associated with them.

This is the global search results provided by SharePoint where you can search data within default or custom properties associated with the results.

Once a user enters any keyword in Search Box Web Part, then results are shown using Search Results Web Part. This web part is used across all the vertical pages (Everything, People, etc.) and results are displayed based on the scope and specific formats for each content type.

Using Search Results Web Part, you can change the query to configure result source to specify specific content to be searched.

Everything	results.aspx	Local SharePoint Results
People	peopleresults.aspx	Local People Results
Conversations	Conversationresults.aspx	Conversations
Videos	videoresults.aspx	Local Video Results

You can also use Advance Mode to define the query, based on Keyword and Property filter. By default, Search Results use a query to get value from Search Box query variable {searchboxquery}.

You can also enhance your queries via

1. Refiners
2. Sorting
3. Settings
4. Test

You can also change settings for display templates. Either you can select default display templates or create custom display template in accordance with your branding requirement.

You can also change other settings like a number of results per page, result count, language drop down, etc.

Figure 1.56 Search Results

5. Taxonomy Refinement Panel

This Web Part helps the user to refine search results on term set data. To use this Web Part, you must also have a Search Data Provider Web Part on this page and use Managed Navigation.

As it's self-explanatory that Taxonomy Refinement Panel Web Part (TRPWP) is more or less similar to Refinement Web Part (RWP) in terms of functionality. Now it's obvious to get confused which web part to use and where?

Let's try to understand the difference between these two web parts and where you can use it?

Refinement Web Part can be used, to filter contents returned via Search results web part. For example, you can filter records based on Author or Modified date. Based on these filters, the contents shown on the page would narrow down the results which help users to see what exactly they are looking for.

Coming back to Taxonomy Refinement Panel Web Part, it also enables users to filter contents shown on the page, however, this web part filters contents using categories derived from sites navigation and it displays category-specific editorial content.

Remember: in order to use Taxonomy Refinement Panel Web Part, we can add only to those sites which use following i.e.

1. **Managed Navigation**
   To define and maintain site navigation by using term sets.

2. **Category pages to display content (faceted navigation)**
   Category pages and Catalog item pages are page layouts that you can use to show Catalog content in a consistent manner across your site.

Again this is quite an advance and a detailed topic which requires various steps like, creating term sets and other configurations to be set. As we proceed further, we would be in comfortable position to implement this web part in our sites.

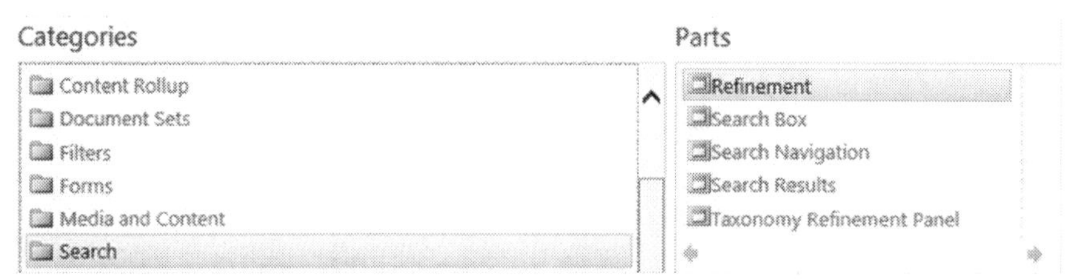

Figure 1.57 Search Web Parts

SEARCH-DRIVEN CONTENT

Search-Driven Content Web Parts provide the same functionalities as Content Search Web Part. Search-Driven Content Web Parts include pre-defined filters that users can use directly on their page.

In order to work with these web parts, we need to configure search results sets along with associated properties (Managed / Crawled).

Search-Driven Content web parts features are as follows

1. Catalog-Item Reuse

Use this Web Part to reuse or republish the content of an item from a catalog.

In SharePoint, **cross-site publishing (XSP)** is a concept where content authored in one site collection can be consumed and published in another site collection.

Another concept is the **catalog**, which allows a SharePoint list to be published to any other site collections. Later, other site collections can connect to this list via catalog and consume that data. The only limitation is that list should be published within the same farm.

2. Items Matching a Tag

This Web Part will show items that are tagged with a term.

When you add it to the page, this Web Part will show items from the current site matching the page navigation context. You can change this setting to show items from another site or list by editing the Web Part and changing its search criteria. You can also specify whether you want the Web Part to display items associated with a different tag instead.

As new content is discovered by search, this Web Part will display an updated list of items each time the page is viewed.

This web part is very useful in rolling up items that have been tagged with managed metadata terms.

3. Pages

This Web Part will show any items that are derived from the Pages content type.

When you add it to the page, this Web Part will show items from the current site. You can change this setting to show items from another site or list by editing the Web Part and changing its search criteria.

As new content is discovered by search, this Web Part will display an updated list of items each time the page is viewed.

This web part shows only .aspx pages.

4. Pictures

This Web Part will show any items that are derived from the Picture or Image content type.

When you add it to the page, this Web Part will show items from the current site. You can change this setting to show items from another site or list by editing the Web Part and changing its search criteria.

As new content is discovered by search, this Web Part will display an updated list of items each time the page is viewed.

This web part is used to display pictures using Slideshow display template. Clicking the link, it takes the user to display form to view properties of that picture.

5. Popular Items

This Web Part will show items that have been recently viewed by many users.

When you add it to the page, this Web Part will show items from the current site. You can change this setting to show items from another site or list by editing the Web Part and changing its search criteria. You can also customize how items are sorted.
As new content is discovered by search, this Web Part will display an updated list of items each time the page is viewed.

6. Recently Changed Items

This Web Part will show items that have been modified recently. This can help site users track the latest activity on a site or a library.

When you add it to the page, this Web Part will show items from the current site. You can change this setting to show items from another site or list by editing the Web Part and changing its search criteria.

As new content is discovered by search, this Web Part will display an updated list of items each time the page is viewed.

7. Recommended Items

This Web Part will show content recommendations based on usage patterns for the current page.

When you add it to the page, this Web Part will show items from the current site. You can change this setting to show items from another site or list by editing the Web Part and changing its search criteria.
As new content is discovered by search, this Web Part will display an updated list of items each time the page is viewed.

8. Videos

This Web Part will show any items that are derived from the Video content type. It will sort items by number of views.

When you add it to the page, this Web Part will show items from the current site. You can change this setting to show items from another site or list by editing the Web Part and changing its search criteria.
As new content is discovered by search, this Web Part will display an updated list of items each time the page is viewed.

This web part only shows videos along with total length for each video. Ideally, you should keep all the videos in an Asset Library to manage these assets effectively.

9. Web Pages

This Web Part will show any items that are derived from the Page content type.

When you add it to the page, this Web Part will show items from the current site. You can change this setting to show items from another site or list by editing the Web Part and changing its search criteria.
As new content is discovered by search, this Web Part will display an updated list of items each time the page is viewed.

10. Wiki Pages

This Web Part will show any items that are derived from the Wiki Page content type.

When you add it to the page, this Web Part will show items from the current site. You can change this setting to show items from another site or list by editing the Web Part and changing its search criteria.

As new content is discovered by search, this Web Part will display an updated list of items each time the page is viewed.

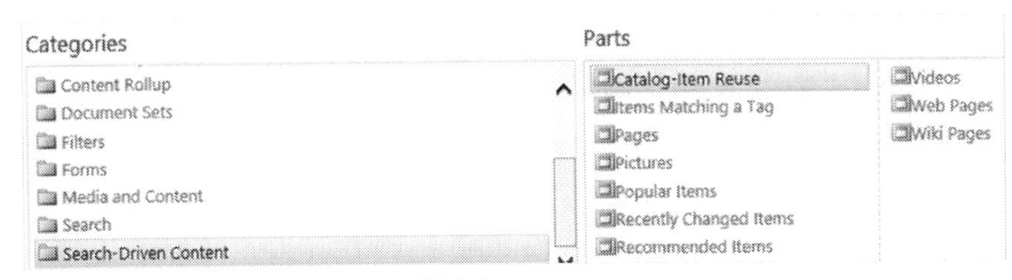

Figure 1.58 Search-Driven Content Web Parts

SOCIAL COLLABORATION

Social Collaboration Web Parts are designed for the social components within the organization like user contact details, shared note board, tag clouds, user tasks, etc.

Social Collaboration web parts features are as follows

1. Contact Details

Displays details about a contact for this page or site.

The user can select any one person using people picker in web part settings. You can also set the properties to display person's picture and Job Title.

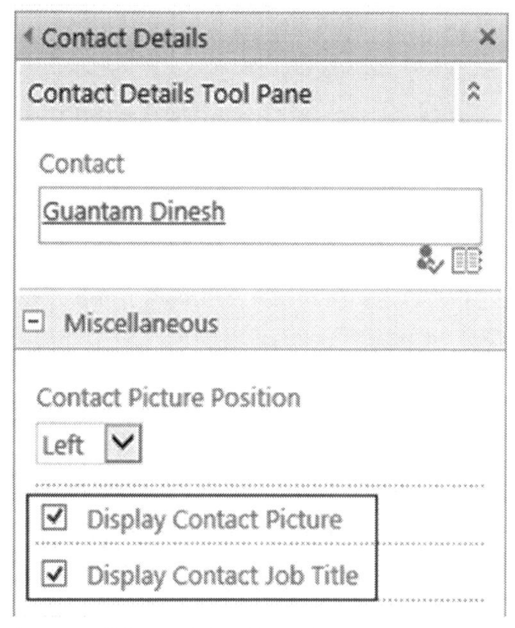

Figure 1.59 Contact Details Tool Pane

After selecting the person and respective properties, the contact details info would be shown on the page.

Figure 1.60 Contact Profile

2. Note Board

Enable users to leave short, publicly-viewable notes about this page.

If you need to have a speedy conversation with your colleagues within your organization but do not wish to engage in a formal discussion board list. In this case with the Note Board Web Part, you can instantly post notes to your SharePoint site.

In order to post a note, you can simply type texts into the text box and click Post. The note will be published instantly. It's also pretty simple to edit or delete the post that was posted by you (as an author).

Note Board

Post

‹ Previous | Next ›

Administrator 10/18/2016 7:11 PM Edit | Delete

Welcome to SharePoint 2016

Figure 1.61 Note Board

To view all the posts, the user can click Previous/Next button to navigate different pages on Note Board.
User also have additional properties to control the behavior of this web part such as

1. Posting limits

User can set the number to show posts

2. Enable new note entry

If unchecked this property then users cannot add a new post. However, the existing posts would be shown

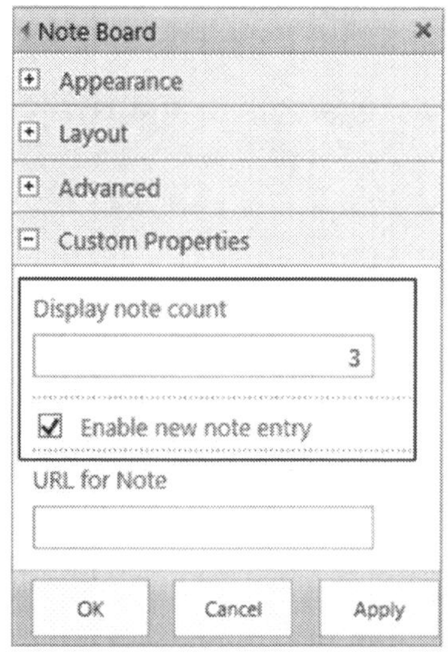

Figure 1.62 Note Board Settings

3. Organization Browser

This Web Part displays each person in the reporting chain in an interactive view optimized for browsing organization charts.

In order to work with Organization Browser Web Part, SharePoint must know who reports to whom. We need to add this detail first to the User Profile.

The Organization Browser uses Manager Field to know who the user reports to and populates the chart.

Users have two choices to view, Silverlight or HTML.

4. Site Users

Use the Site Users Web Part to see a list of the site users and their online status.

Site Users Web Part shows the name of the users in a specific SharePoint group or all groups on a site. If already integrated with Skype for Business (Lync), users can quickly see people's online presence as well.

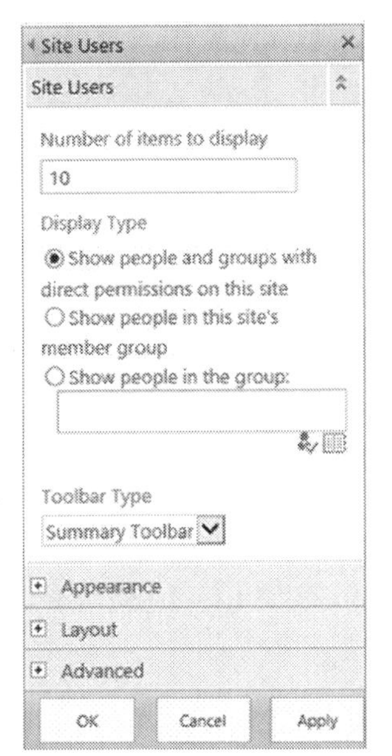

Figure 1.63 Site Users Settings

Figure 1.64 Site Users

5. Tag Cloud

Displays the most popular subjects being tagged inside your organization.

Tag Cloud Web Part shows all those tags pertaining to the current user or by all other users. This web part enables the team members to see the tags they collectively use to tag relevant content.

The user can set properties to show tags by current users, all users or all users for current URL. The user can also set maximum items to display (default 50) along with a count to be shown on the page.

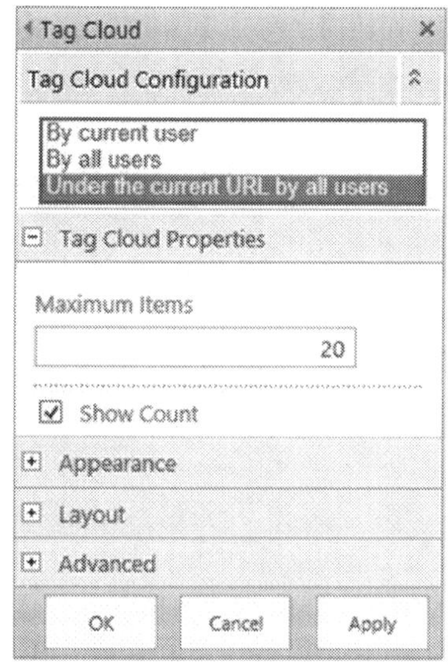

Figure 1.65 Tag Cloud Configuration

6. User Tasks

Displays tasks that are assigned to the current user.

User Tasks Web Part shows all the tasks for the currently logged in user. All tasks that are assigned to the logged-in user for the current website.

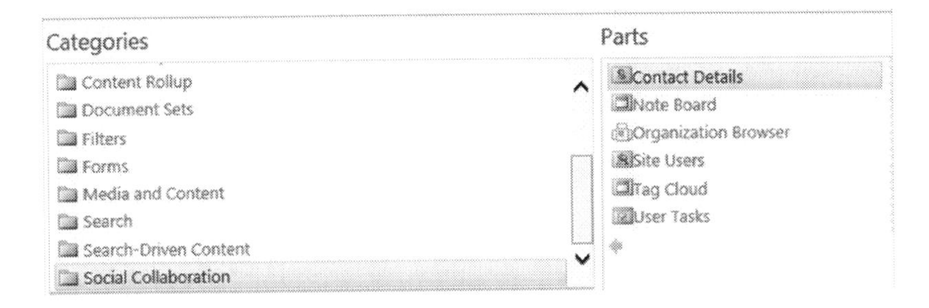

Figure 1.66 Social Collaboration Web Parts

Summary:

This chapter provided basic knowledge about the out-of-the-box web parts available in SharePoint 2016 and how you can use them to provide various services to your organization, develop more efficient business processes, and engage people with the information required to make informed business decisions. After reading this chapter, you should also better understand the core components of SharePoint, including lists, libraries, and various web part categories.

Develop It Yourself – Exercises 1.0

You must have got a fair idea about OOTB web parts. It's time for setting up a development environment to implement fantastic features. First thing first!!!

1. Create a Site collection (Main)
2. Create a Team subsite under main site collection
3. List down two important features of SharePoint 2016 for your organization and why?

To get step-by-step instructions of exercises 1.0, visit our site.

DIY

CHAPTER 2: OUT-OF-THE-BOX WEB PARTS IN ACTION

In this section, we will be looking at few of the widely used web parts. By the end of this section, you should be able to use these web parts with less or no configuration at all. Let's buckle down to implement fascinating OOTB functionalities.

CALENDAR

Calendar web part is used, to display data in a calendar view. In previous versions of SharePoint (2010 and before), there was a separate web part but SharePoint 2013 onwards, you can add this web part using APPS category.

Calendar web part can be used to display data from any task lists. Furthermore, you can use any other custom list, having at least two date columns and one text column. These two dates can be used to set start date, end date and text field column can be used to set different headers available for this web part.

For example, let's create two lists, namely User Tasks and Holiday using Task and custom list template respectively.

User Tasks:
User Tasks list derived from Task list template, so there are already two date columns available i.e. Start Date and Due Date and Title column can be used to show Task title in the calendar view.

For demo purpose, I added two entries which assigned to logged-in user i.e. Administrator.

Task Name		Description	Due Date	Assigned To
Setup SharePoint 2016 Tutorial ※	•••	Need to setup the enviroment	October 31	Administrator
Task assigned to Me ※	•••		December 31	Administrator

Figure 2.1 Task List

Holidays

Let's create another custom list called Holiday to store company holidays. You can use this list, to show holidays details, using calendar view for end users.

Once you create a new custom list, Title column is added by default so we just need to add two columns (say Start Date and End Date). Post creating these columns, add few sample entries to the list. It may look like as shown below.

Title		Start Date	End Date
Thanksgiving Day ※	•••	11/24/2016	10/24/2016
Day after Thanksgiving Day ※	•••	11/25/2016	11/25/2016
Christmas Eve ※	•••	12/24/2016	12/24/2016
Christmas Day ※	•••	12/25/2016	12/25/2016

Figure 2.2 Holidays Custom List

Next, we will create a new view, based on Calendar view for our custom list (Holidays). Select Holidays list and click "Create view" using quick menu

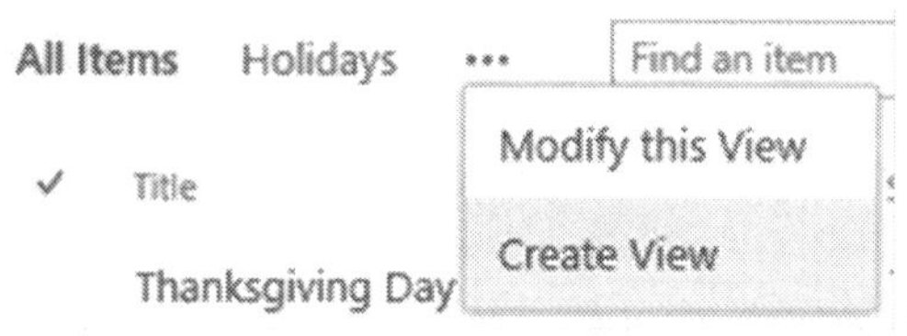

Figure 2.3 Create a View

You will be redirected to a page with available view type. There are four types of view available

1. Standard view 2. Datasheet view 3. Calendar view 4. Gantt view

Click Calendar View type link

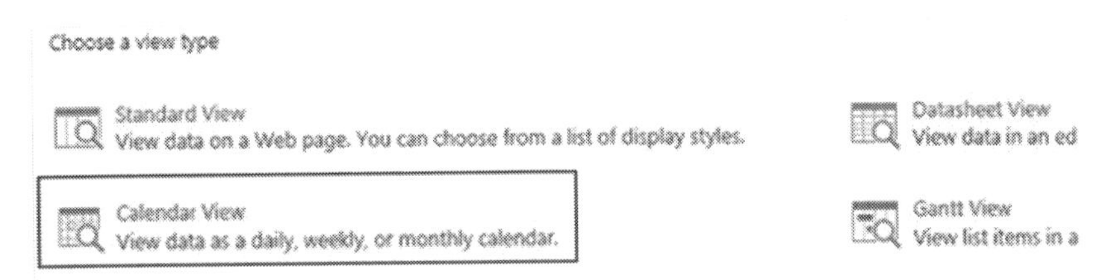

Figure 2.4 View Type Options

Set following properties for view

1. Name: *Holidays*
2. Time Interval
   a. Begin: From drop down list, select *Start Date*
   b. End: From drop down list, select *End Date*
3. Calendar Columns
   a. Month View Title: From drop down list, select *Title*
   b. Week View Title: From drop down list, select *Title*
   c. Day View Title: From drop down list, select *Title*
4. Default Scope
   a. Select *Month* (radio button)

Click OK to proceed.

Now we are ready to use this view within Calendar Web Part.

Note

We can use web parts in any pages. For simplicity, you can use default.aspx or Home page of SharePoint.

Now navigate to default.aspx (Home). Select "Settings" button from top ribbon.

Figure 2.5 Edit Page menu Option

While editing the page, you can see various zones (Header, Center, Footer, etc.) where you can add a web part. Click "Add a Web Part" from Header section.

You will be shown Web Part Categories and associated web parts for that group. Select "Apps" from category and select "Holidays" as shown below. Click Add button to proceed.

Figure 2.6 Apps → Holidays

The data are shown in this web part using the default view set to that list. You need to change the view for this web part. Select down arrow from the top right and click "Edit Web Part".

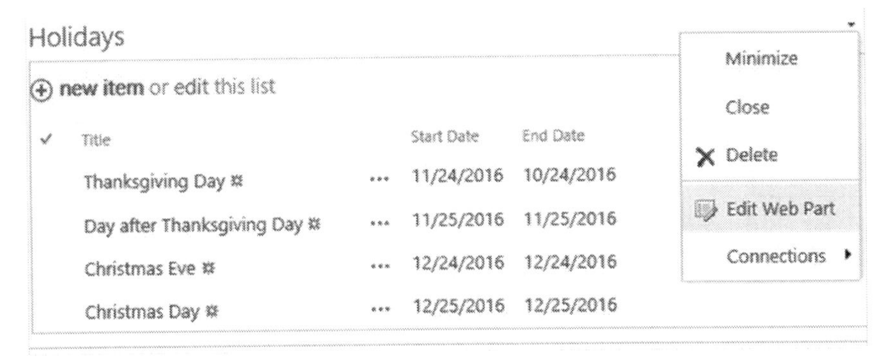

Figure 2.7 Edit List Web Part

Using Web Part Settings panel, select view for this Web part

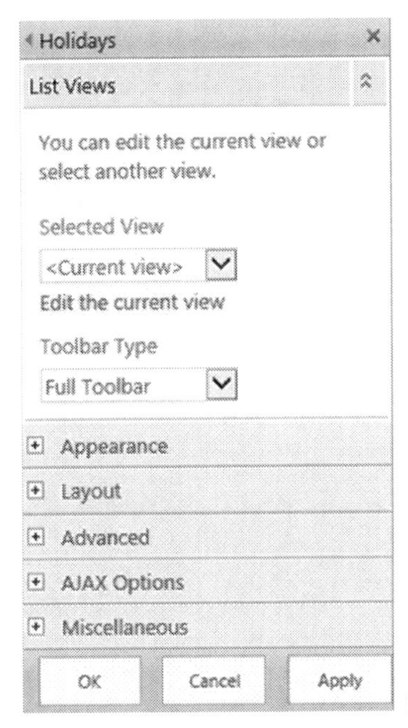

Figure 2.8 List Web Part Properties

In Selected View section, click *<Current view>* drop down list and select Holidays view that we just created previously.

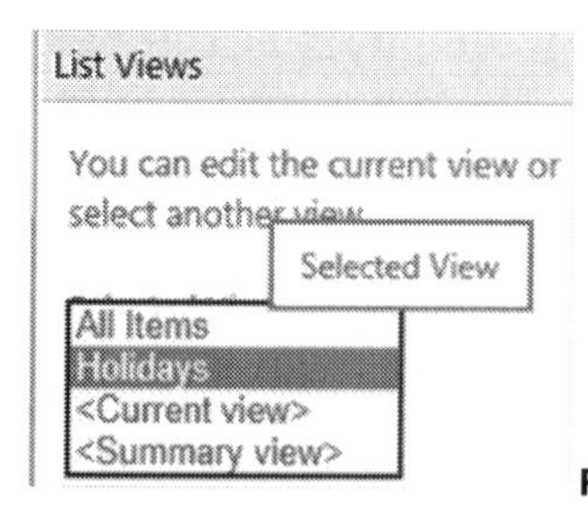

Figure 2.9 Change View For Custom List

Toolbar Type: *No Toolbar (It will not allow to add or update list items)*

In Appearance section, you can set other attributes like height, width and Chrome type. Set the desired height and width as per the layout.

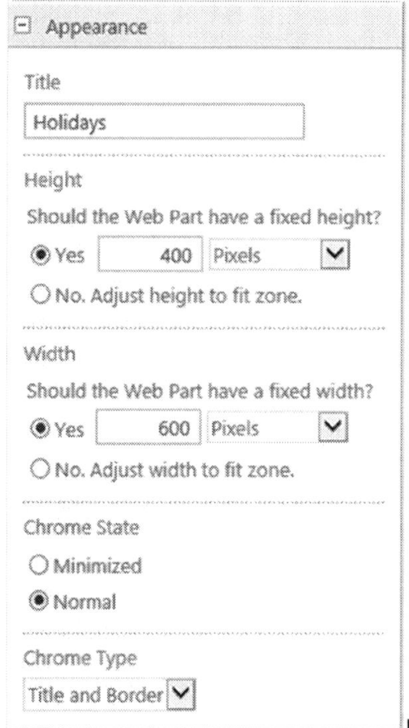

Figure 2.10 Appearance Section

We will proceed with other values which are set by default. Click OK.
Save the page, check-in and publish the page using top ribbon.

Figure 2.11 Commit Changes

Congratulations!!! You have just added your first web part successfully.

Holidays

December 2016

SUNDAY	MONDAY	TUESDAY	WEDNESDAY	THURSDAY	FRIDAY	SATURDAY
27	28	29	30	1	2	3
4	5	6	7	8	9	10
11	12	13	14	15	16	17
18	19	20	21	22	23	24 12:00 am - 12 Christmas Eve
25 12:00 am - 12:0 Christmas Day	26	27	28	29	30	31

Figure 2.12 Calendar View for Custom List

Upcoming Holidays

In our first exercise, we learned how to use Calendar view in Apps web part. We can use the same Holidays list to display data in a simpler manner.

Let's start with editing the same page.

1. Click "Add Web Part Link" from Right zone
2. From "Apps" category, select Holidays list
3. Click on down arrow from newly added list web part - Holidays [2]
4. As mentioned earlier, the default view for this list would be the selected to display data using this web part
5. Click on the link "Edit the current view"
6. Set the view settings properties in Columns section
   a. Title (linked to item) – 1
   b. Start Date – 2

a number in the Position from left box.

Display	Column Name	Position from Left
☑	Title (linked to item)	1
☑	Start Date	2

Figure 2.13 Column Ordering

7. In Filters section, set the Start date is greater than or equal to today

Note

We applied this filter so that only upcoming holidays will be shown to the users.

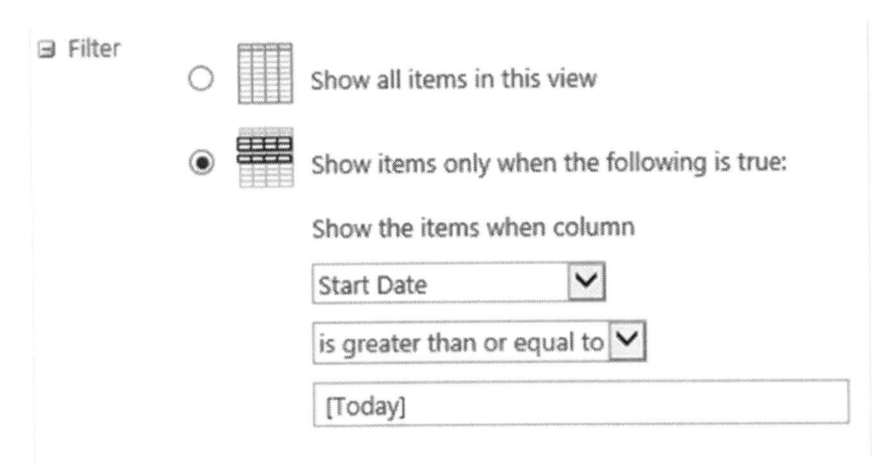

Figure 2.14 Filter Options

8. In Tabular view section, uncheck Allow individual item checkboxes

Tabular View ☑ Allow individual item checkboxes

Figure 2.15 Tabular View

9. For style, select Newsletter view style

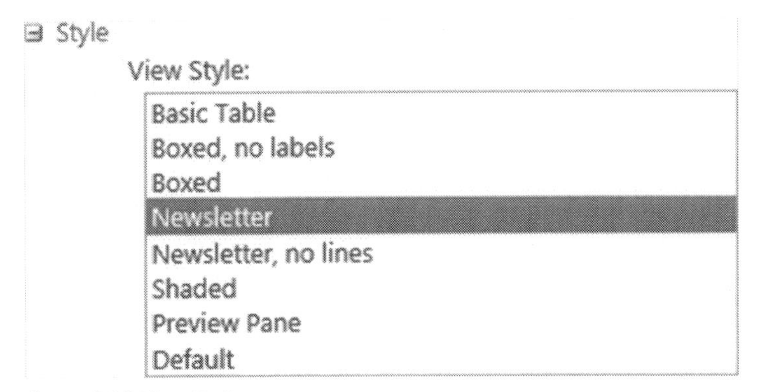

Figure 2.16 View Style

10. You can restrict the number of items to be shown.
    In Item Limits, type 3

Figure 2.17 Item Limit

11. Click OK.

We are now done with view settings, start setting up other web part properties. Click "Edit Web Part".

12. Set Toolbar type to "No Toolbar"

13. In Appearance section change Title to "Upcoming Holidays"

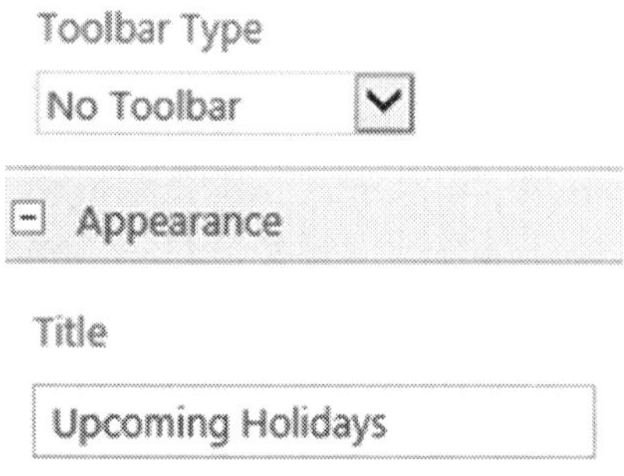

Figure 2.18 Set Title

14. Click OK to save the changes.

Well Done!!! You just added new web part using the same list.

Upcoming Holidays

Title	Start Date
Thanksgiving Day NEW	11/24/2016
Day after Thanksgiving Day NEW	11/25/2016
Christmas Eve NEW	12/24/2016

1 - 3 ▸

Figure 2.19 Upcoming Holidays Listing

Note

Since we defined 3 item limit, SharePoint added paging buttons automatically.

RSS FEEDS

Using RSS feeds web part, you can display contents from any external site (Feed publisher). This is a great way to get the latest information from an external site by adding the RSS Viewer Web Part to a page on your site.

For example, you can use RSS Viewer Web Part to display information such as recently published articles by Microsoft. In this example, we will be using RSS feed provided by Microsoft.

Feed URL: https://support.microsoft.com/en-us/rss?rssid=18618

Note

In order to use RSS Feed web part, we MUST have URL for the RSS feed.

You can get additional feeds from Microsoft site: https://support.microsoft.com/en-us/gp/selectrss?target=rss&c1=505&=GSSProdSelMore505

Add RSS Viewer Web Part

You can add web part using the same steps

1. Edit the page to add the new web part.
2. Click "Add a Web Part" from zone where you want this web part to display
3. Under Categories, click Content Rollup. Under Web Parts, click RSS Viewer Web Part, and finally click Add

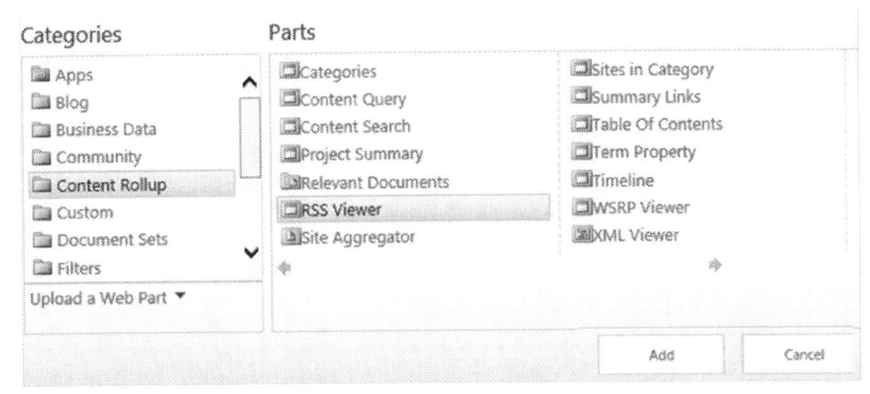

Figure 2.20 Configure RSS Viewer Web Part

After adding this web part, it shows a message "***You have not selected an RSS feed. Please Open the tool pane to set the feed url.***"

You have not selected an RSS feed. Please Open the tool pane to set the feed url.

Figure 2.21 Tool Pane

1. Click "Open the tool pane" to set the web part properties.

→ Alternatively, you can set properties via clicking "Edit Web Part".

2. In Appearance section
   a. Set Title to "Knowledge Base - SP 2016"

   b. Set Chrome type – "Title and Border" from drop down list

3. In RSS Properties section
   a. Set RSS Feed URL to https://support.microsoft.com/en-us/rss?rssid=18618

   b. Set Feed refresh time (in minutes) to 10

   → Default value is 120 but you can configure it as per your requirement.

c. Set Feed Limit to 3

→ Default value is 5 but you can set this limit as per your design layout.

d. Click OK

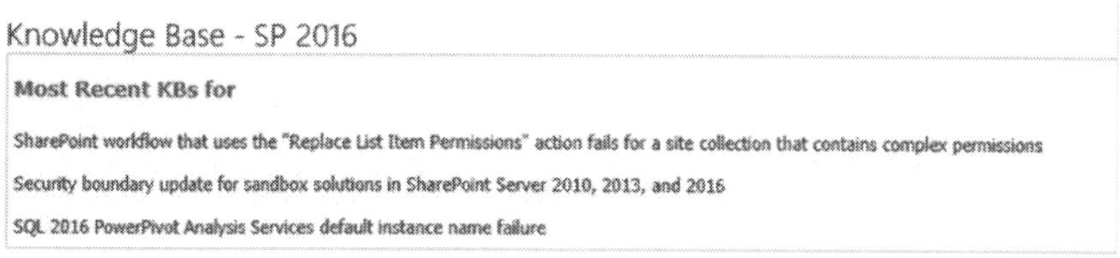

Knowledge Base - SP 2016

Most Recent KBs for

SharePoint workflow that uses the "Replace List Item Permissions" action fails for a site collection that contains complex permissions

Security boundary update for sandbox solutions in SharePoint Server 2010, 2013, and 2016

SQL 2016 PowerPivot Analysis Services default instance name failure

Figure 2.22 RSS Viewer Output

Great!!! Now, all our users will be able to get latest KB articles without any further configuration. This is a great example of no code solution.

That's what I call **"Power of OOTB"**

TASK / SUBTASKS

Using Share Point 2016, you can make a great use of Task Lists to manage project tasks. Task list template, provides the ability to add multiple subtasks to tasks list along with other features such as an indent or outdent a task, move a task up or down in the list, or permanently delete a task from the list.

The timeline is a functionality, taken from MS project server, to display a timeline of the Tasks. Users have the ability to display or remove tasks or subtasks from the timeline.

You can achieve various functionalities on a task list

1. Create new Task
2. Delete a Task
3. Timeline with the start and end dates
4. Create Subtasks
5. Indent
6. Task Views

In this section, we will create a Project Tasks list to manage tasks for various projects (category). Let's start...

The very first step is to add an APP. From Settings icon ⚙, click "Add an app"

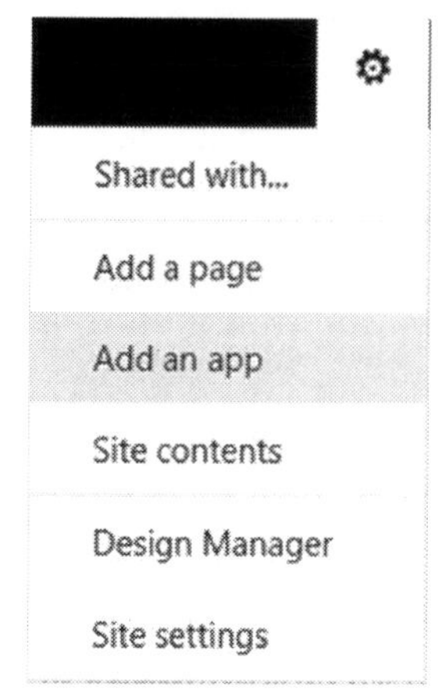

Figure 2.23 Add an App

Click "Tasks" template and set its Name to "Project Tasks"

Figure 2.24 Templates

Modify the schema of Task list

As mentioned earlier, we need to create tasks for various projects (categories) so we will add a new column to this list.

You need to go to Project Tasks lists setting via top ribbon menu

Figure 2.25 List Settings

In columns section, click "Create column" link

Set the following properties for the column

1. Name – Project
2. Data type - Choice (menu to choose from)
3. Set the values for "Type each choice on a separate line:"
   a. Finance
   b. Human Resource
   c. Information Technology
   d. Marketing
4. Click OK

Our Project Tasks list is ready to use and it will look like as shown below

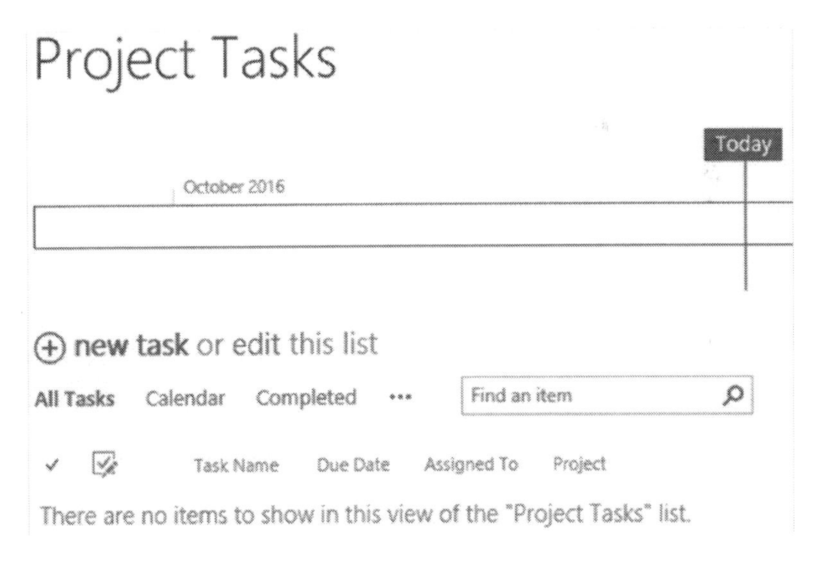

Figure 2.26 Project Task List

Add a new task

1. Click New task
2. Create three items as shown below

Figure 2.27 Task Items

Add new subtask to an existing task

1. Click on eclipse menu (...) for 1st task (Welcome mail to all new joiners"

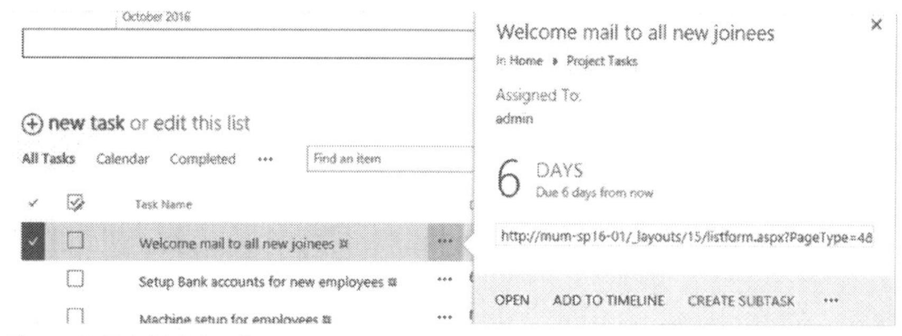

Figure 2.28 Add Subtask

2. Add following details to new subtask and click on link "stop editing this list"

3. A new subtask has been added below the first task. You can see an arrow added before task denoting that it has subtasks under it.

Figure 2.29 Task / Subtask View

Multi-level Task list

You can easily create a multi-level task list, either by clicking a task or a subtask and open its menu to add the subtask.

Once you've finished, you will have a multi-level task list that contains a hierarchy of tasks and subtasks.

Indent and Outdent buttons

Using these buttons, you can

1. Change the level of a subtask and move it up to the same level (or higher) of its parent task
2. Change the level of a subtask and move it down to a lower level

Change the parent of a subtask

Using Move up / Move Down button, you can change the parent of any subtasks. This is a great functionality to manage your tasks quickly and efficiently.

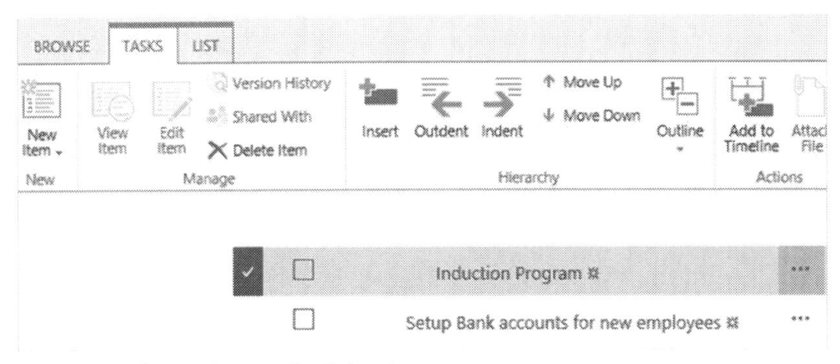

Figure 2.30 Change Parent of a Subtask

Add task to TimeLine

Click on eclipse menu (...) on any task and click "ADD TO TIMELINE" link

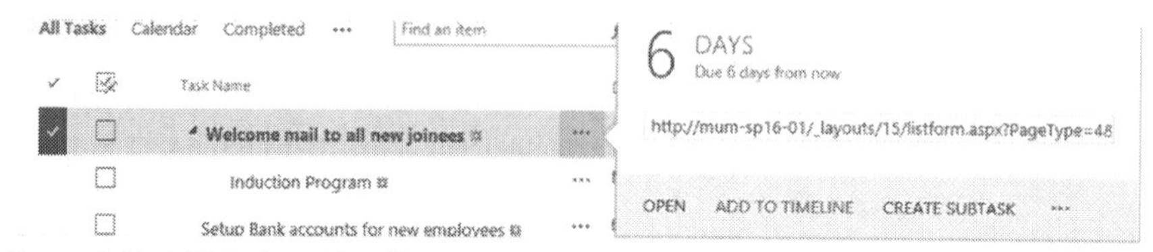

Figure 2.31 Add Task to Timeline

Once you add the task to Timeline, it will appear in Timeline web part as shown below.

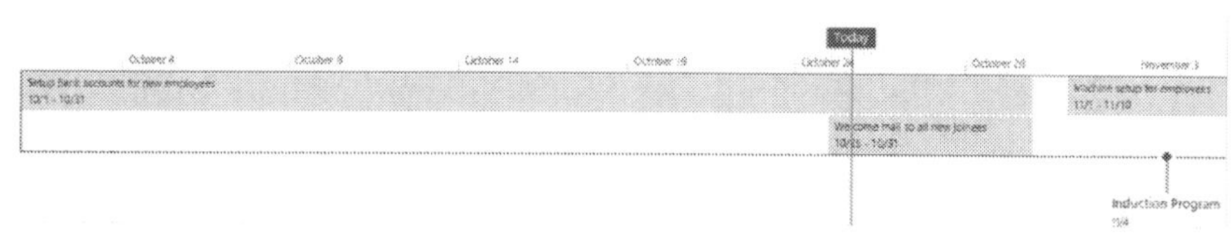

Figure 2.32 Timeline View

Remove task from TimeLine

You can remove the task from a timeline which has been added to the timeline. To remove the task from Timeline, Click on eclipse menu (...) on existing task and click "REMOVE FROM TIMELINE" link.

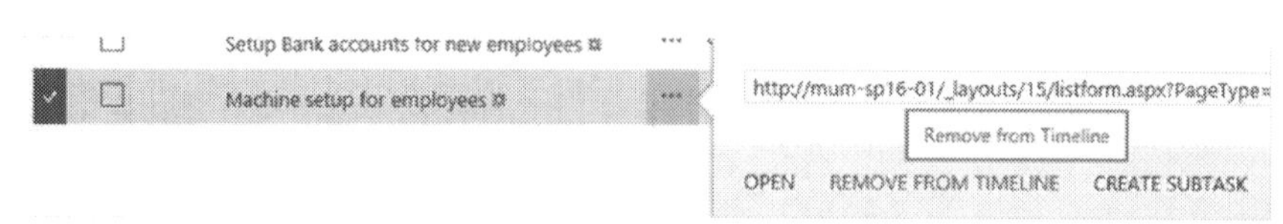

Figure 2.33 Remove Task from Timeline

Hiding TimeLine

If you decide not to show Timeline then you can do it quickly via these steps,

1. Edit the page (Settings → Edit page)

2. Select the Project Tasks list web part and click "Edit Web Part"

3. In List Views section, uncheck "Show timeline"

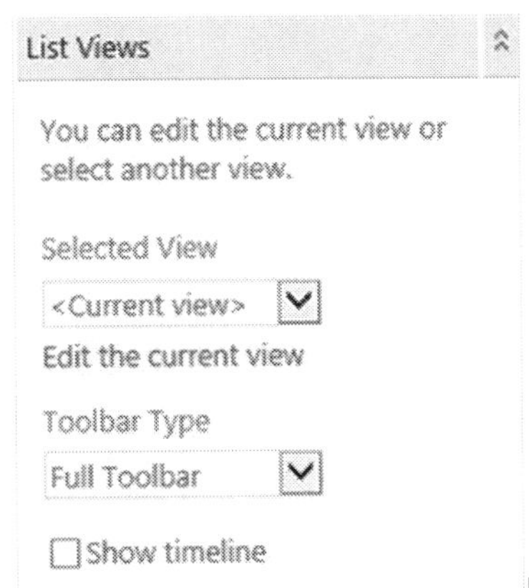

Figure 2.34 List View Properties

Formatting the TimeLine Display

A Very cool feature of the timeline that allows you to Color the tasks. You can select a task and click on Timeline. A new tab TIMELINE appears using which you can format the selected task with color, font and highlight color.

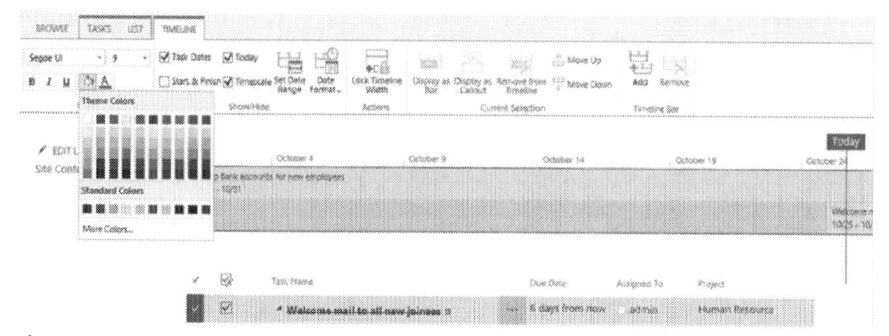

Figure 2.35 TimeLine Display Formatting

Task list Views

By default, there are additional views to display task details. There are following views available for Task list.

Note

If needed we can create new views as well. For example, to show tasks as per the Project.

1. *All Tasks* - Consolidated view for all tasks

2. Calendar view displays tasks in calendar view with start date and end date.

TUESDAY	WEDNESDAY	THURSDAY
27	28	29
4	5	6
Setup Bank accounts for new employees		
11	12	13
Setup Bank accounts for new employees		
18	19	20
Setup Bank accounts for new employees		
25	26	27
Setup Bank accounts for new employees		
Welcome mail to all		

Figure 2.36 Tasks in Calendar View

3. Another view is to display all the tasks which are completed (% complete)

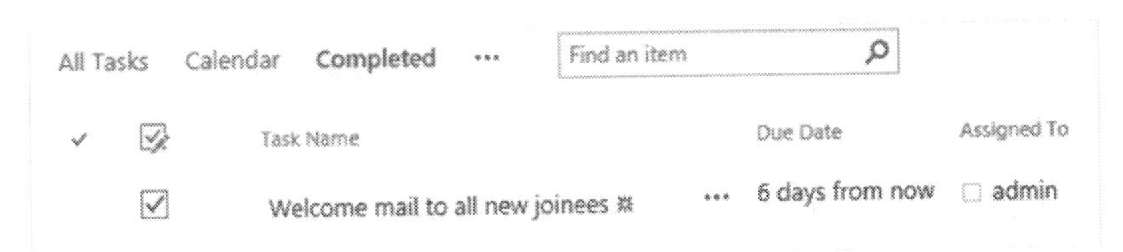

Figure 2.37 Tasks Based On Status

4. Gantt Chart

Figure 2.38 Gantt Chart View

5. Late Tasks (Incomplete task where the due date is less than today)

6. My Tasks (Assigned to logged-in user)

7. Upcoming (Incomplete task where the due date is greater than today)

Hooray!!! Now, we can say proudly, Task Management couldn't be easier. Say "adieu" to your hand-written notes, excel or "To-Do" type application to manage daily tasks using SharePoint.

BLOG / DISCUSSION

In this section, we will learn more about the discussion board feature provided by SharePoint 2016. This is one of the best collaboration tools to engage teams and users using Discussion board app. In general, Discussion Board is a list with specially formatted views.

Let's start... Go to Site Contents using Site settings icon

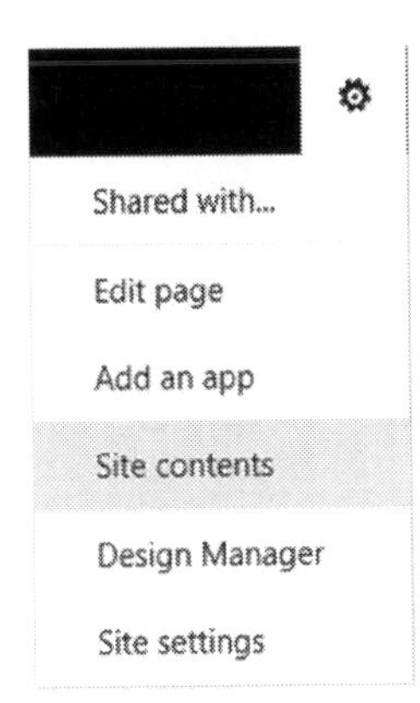

Figure 2.39 Site Contents

Click "Add an app"

Type "discussion" in search app. You should be able to view "Discussion Board" in the results pane.

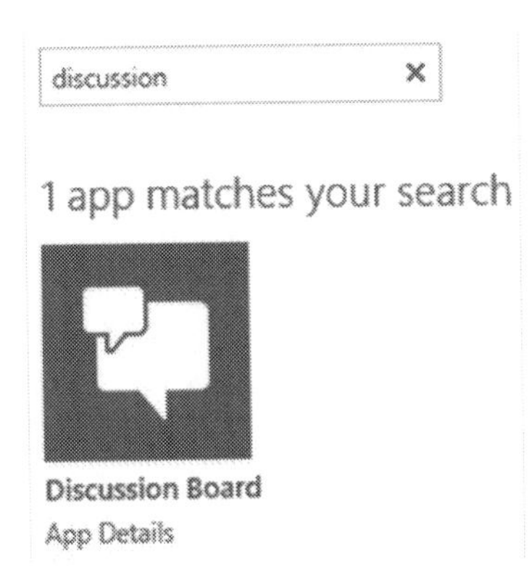

Figure 2.40 Select Discussion App

Click "Discussion Board" and provide a name "*SharePoint Discussion*". Once created (as mentioned earlier) it is just a specially formatted list which comes with few specialized views to get you started.

Now create a new discussion and set subject line to "*SharePoint 2016 Features Demo*". In body text, type "*SharePoint 2016 includes very exciting features that we will be demonstrating in upcoming demo. Reply to this thread whoever wants to join this session*"

In this case, since it isn't a question so do not check the question box. Marking as a question, it allows you to do some filtering later between questions and non-question discussions.

Click "Save".

Subject *
SharePoint 2016 Features Demo
Body
SharePoint 2016 includes very exciting features that we will be demonstrating in upcoming demo.
Reply to this thread whoever wants to join this session!!!
Question
I am asking a question and want to get answers from other members.
Save Cancel

Figure 2.41 Add a New Discussion

We just created a new discussion for all users to view and respond to this post accordingly.

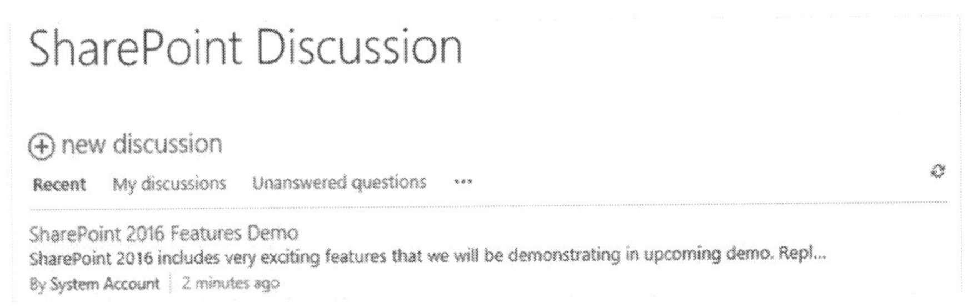

Figure 2.42 Discussion Listing

Let's add a new discussion for a Question type. Click New Discussion. In Subject line and body type "Are you Ready for SharePoint 2016". Mark it as a Question via checking the checkbox.

You can see two discussions in "Recent" views, out of which one is a question and other one is not.

Users can view these discussions and reply accordingly to each post. Any discussion that is created by you, you can mark any reply as the best reply. Best reply always sits on top for that discussion thread. Additionally, you as an author of discussion also can mark it answered if that discussion was a question.

You can also mark any discussion as Featured that will be shown in Featured view

By default, there are five views initially shown to all users i.e.

1. Recent – Added, modified recently
2. What's Hot – Most replied and liked
3. My Discussions – Discussions created by Logged-in user
4. Unanswered questions
5. Answered questions
6. Featured – Marked a featured

Discussion Board list also consists of social features such as "Ratings" and "Like", which provide a personal touch to each reply. Though these features aren't enabled by default but you can enable it using list settings properties.

Go to "SharePoint Discussion" List settings

Figure 2.43 List Settings

Under General settings, click Rating settings

You can see, there are two properties.

1. Allow items in this list to be rated?
Set it to **Yes**

2. Which voting/rating experience you would like to enable for this list?
Select **Likes**

Click OK

Allow items in this list to be rated?

◉ Yes ○ No

Which voting/rating experience you would like to enable for this list?

◉ Likes ○ Star Ratings

Figure 2.44 Ratings Settings

After enabling this feature, users will be able to like the post in their reply ☺

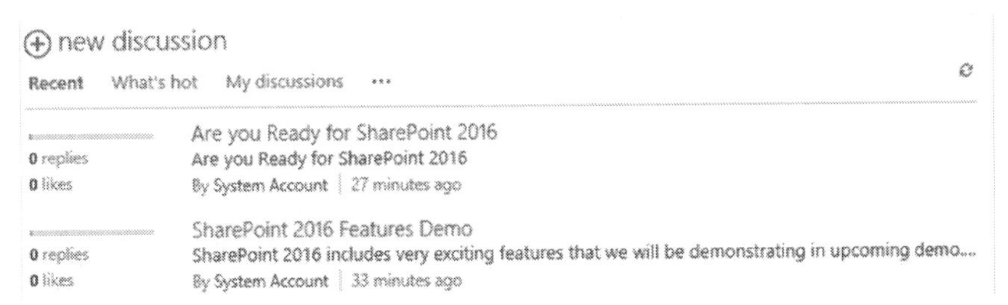

Figure 2.45 Discussion Listing with Ratings

Users can reply to any discussion via clicking on a discussion. You can click "Like" to show a positive gesture. If any thread already liked by you then you can "Unlike" as well.

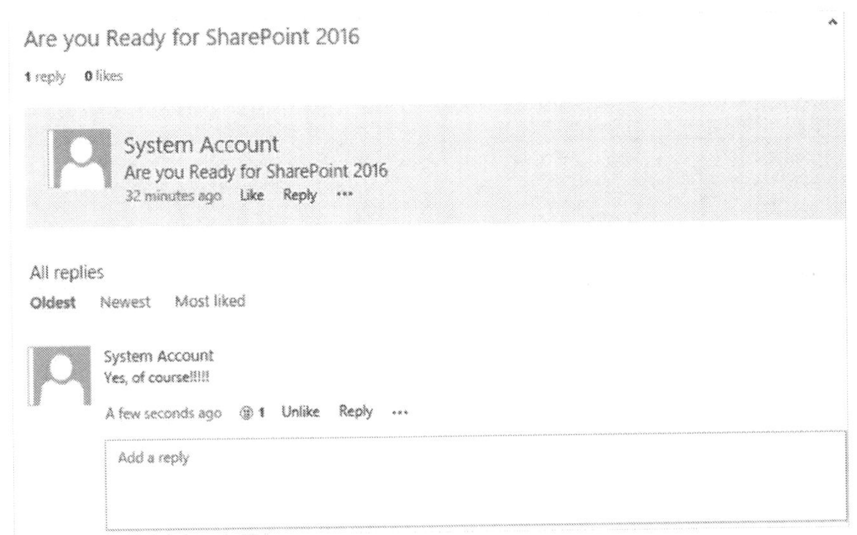

Figure 2.46 Discussion Detailed View

To make any thread Featured, click on eclipse menu (...) and mark as Featured / Unfeatured.

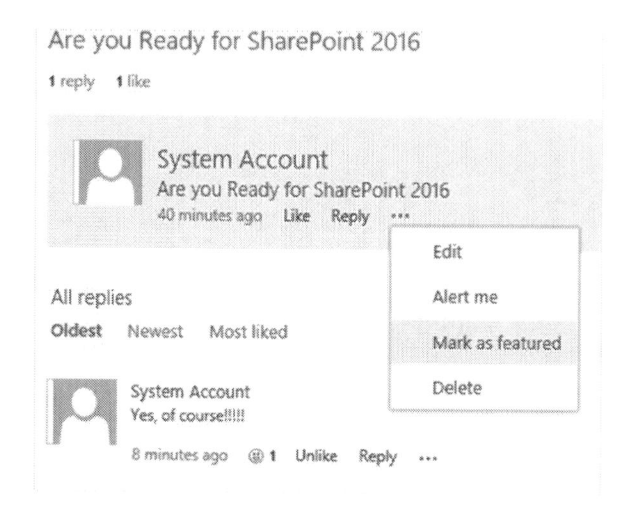

Figure 2.47 Marking as Featured

After marking, this discussion will be shown in Featured view list.

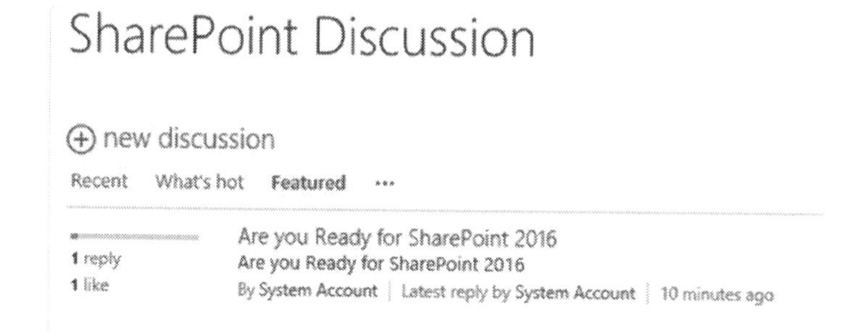

Figure 2.48 Featured View

Apart from above functionalities, you can also add your own metadata using columns. Under the list tab, click on the drop-down menu next to "create column" and choose management. This management view shows you the data as a list.

→ *Open tab "List" from top ribbon. Under Current view section, select "Management"*

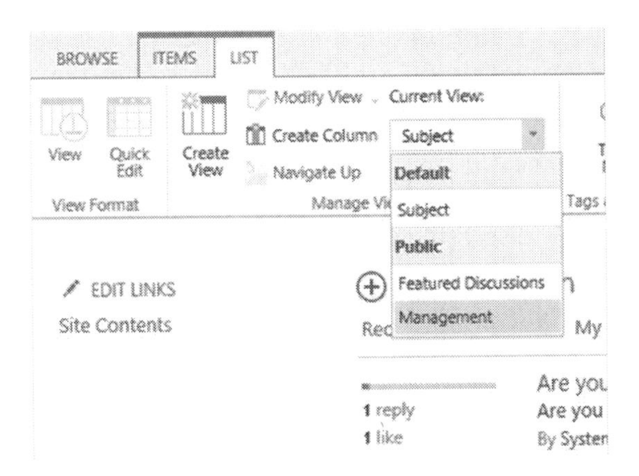

Figure 2.49 Select View Options

Go to the list settings and create a column. For this example, I created a new column called "Category" of type menu with three values "Blog", "Demo" and "Discussion".

Once you add a new column, it automatically appears in new discussion form.

Subject * SharePoint 2016 Features

Body This blog will cover SharePoint 2016 features in details. It will also consist of useful links to knowledge base articals, videos and PDF books.

Question I am asking a question and want to get answers from other members.

Category Blog

Save Cancel

Figure 2.50 Discussion Form with Custom Column

You can extend this functionality, by creating a custom view, based on category or group by category. For this example, I created a new view (Discussion Group) to group it by Category.

This is a great way to display discussion topics by category to all users with a bird's eye view.

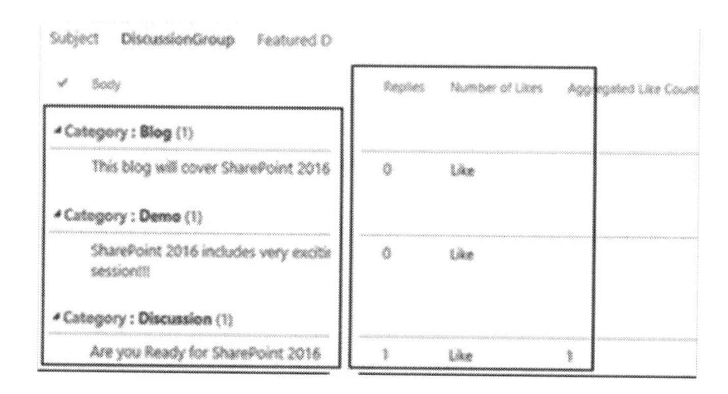

Figure 2.51 Discussion Summary

Another important feature is the ability to connect to Outlook. On List menu, click 'Connect to Outlook'. You can open Outlook and contribute to any of the discussions created in SharePoint. You can see discussion listing right below the inbox. To view all the replies, you need to expand the discussion in outlook.

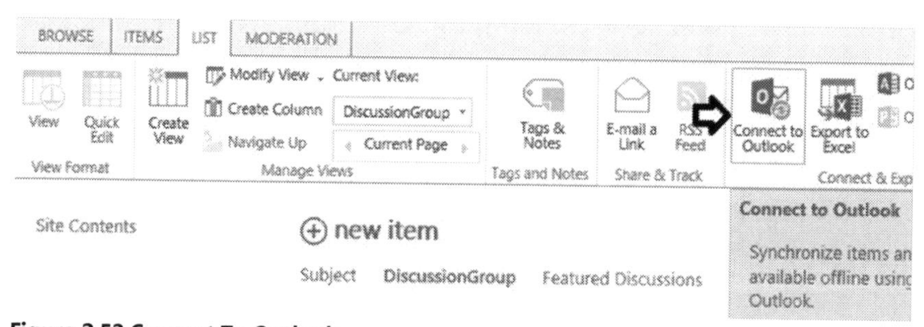

Figure 2.52 Connect To Outlook

In order to reply, select a discussion and on the toolbar, click post reply. The reply is a two-way sync back to SharePoint.

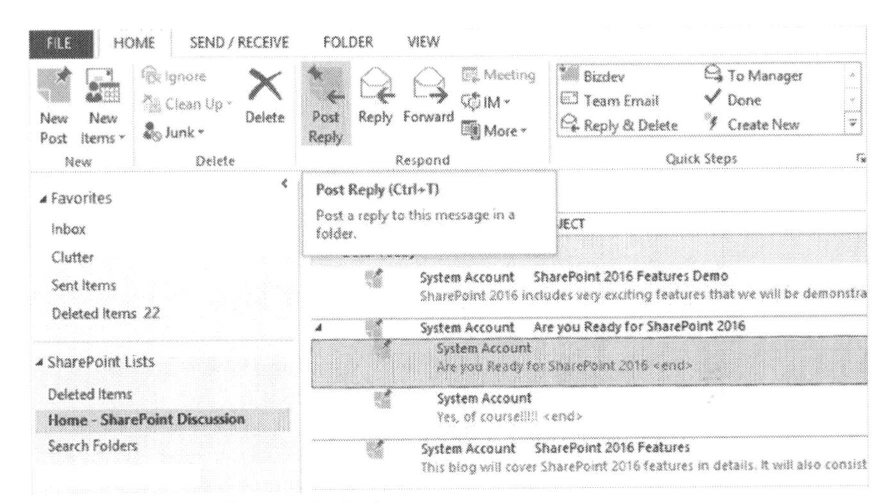

Figure 2.53 Post Reply From Outlook

WOW!!! We just saw that discussion boards are so useful. If you need to post something immediately on your home page to facilitate engagement within your team then there is no other way to achieve this functionality so easily, quickly and efficiently.

CONTENT QUERY WEB PART

The Content Query Web Part (CQWP) is a very handy tool to create an aggregated list based on multiple lists or libraries, either from within a single site or from across a site collection.

For example, you can display a list of links (pointing to respective document) for all document libraries across site collection OR suppose you have any master list on the top-level site in your SharePoint portal and you need to display only filtered records based on some criteria on a subsite then Content Query Web Part is the best answer.

Note

The Content Query Web Part is supported in publishing sites only. Also, the site collection that contains the site must have the publishing features enabled. By default, publishing feature is not activated and you MUST activate the publishing features.

Activate Publishing Features

Go to **Site settings** using Site settings icon 

In Site Collection Administration section, click **Site collection features**

On Site Collection Features page, click **Activate** button next to **SharePoint Server Publishing Infrastructure**.

Figure 2.54 Publishing Infrastructure Feature

Post activation of this feature, you are good to use Content Query Web Part throughout the site collection.

Note

There could be a scenario where this Feature may be turned on or off on each site. In that case, you must activate the SharePoint Server Publishing site feature on each site/subsite where you need to use Content Query Web Part.

Go to **Site settings** using Site settings icon 

In Site Actions section, click **Manage site features**

On Site Features page, click **Activate** for SharePoint Server Publishing.

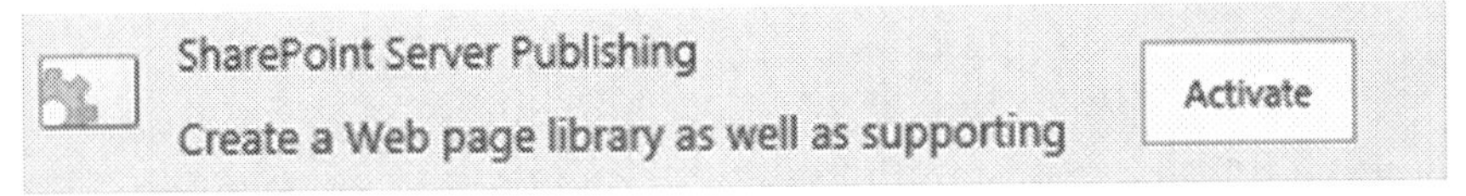

Figure 2.55 Publishing Feature

It's very important to keep in mind that whenever there is some missing tool or feature then you need to verify whether or not the respective features are activated.

In this section, I'll walk you through, how to add Content Query Web Part to SharePoint site, as well as, how to configure Web Part and display roll-up data.

1. Edit the page (Settings → Edit page)
2. Click "Add a Web Part" from a content zone where you want this web part
3. Under "Content Rollup" category, select Content Query Web Part

4. Click Add button

5. Click "open the tool pane" link. You can also select arrow and "Edit Web Part" using web part properties.

6. Under **Content Query Tool Part**, in **Query** section check "Show items from the following list:"

7. Click "**Browse...**" button

8. A new popup window will open, Select "**SharePoint Discussion**" list that we created in the previous section

9. Click OK

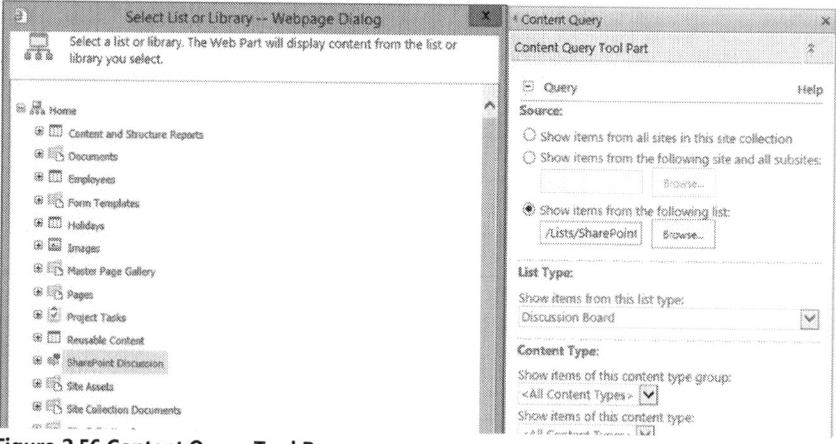

Figure 2.56 Content Query Tool Pane

10. Under Presentation section, set the value 3 for "**Limit the number of items to display Item limit:**"

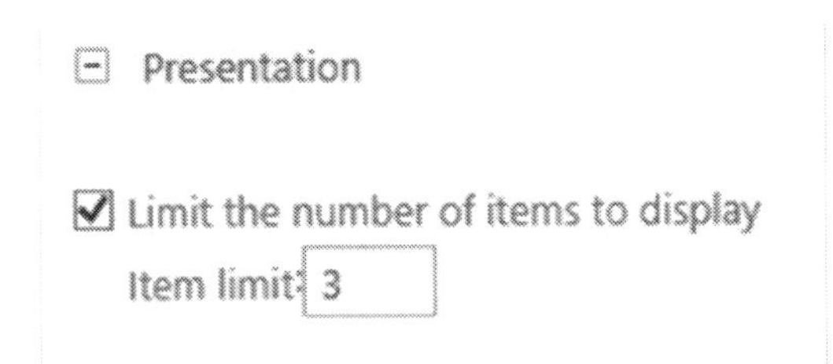

Figure 2.57 Item Limit

11. In Style section, set Group style: Larger text
12. Set Item style: Title with background

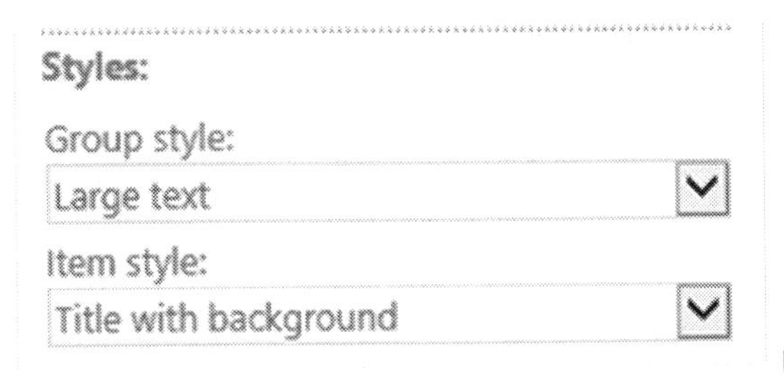

Figure 2.58 CQWP Styles

13. Under Appearance section, set **Title** to "**SharePoint Discussion**"

14. Set **Chrome Type** to "**Title and Border**"

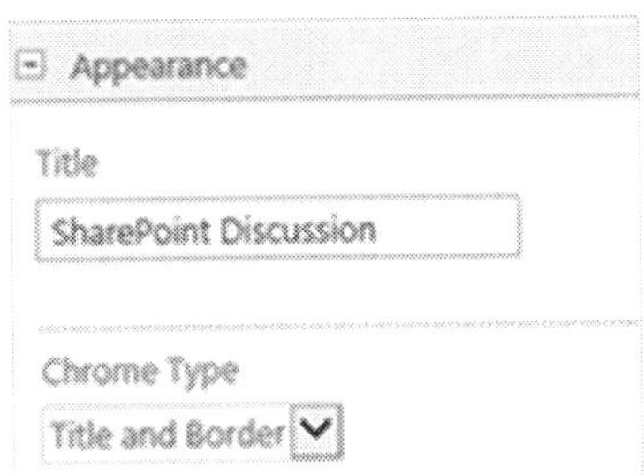

Figure 2.59 CQWP Appearance

15. Click OK

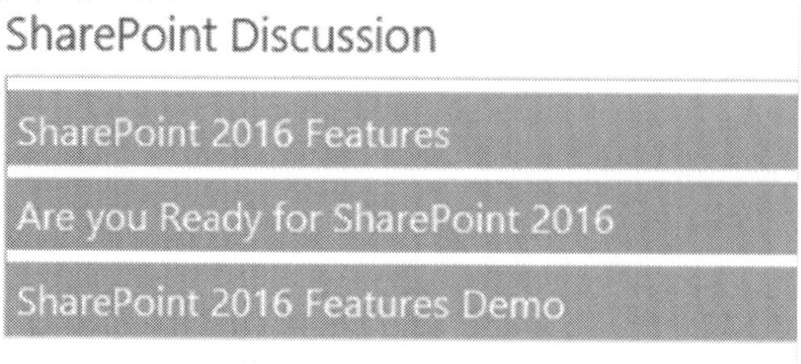

SharePoint Discussion

SharePoint 2016 Features

Are you Ready for SharePoint 2016

SharePoint 2016 Features Demo

Figure 2.60 Content Query Web Part output

That's all!!! Using Content Query Web Part, you can display data using OOTB style template with ease and without any hassle. You can also set additional properties like Replies count, like counts, image, etc. using map properties section.

Summary:

This chapter provided detailed knowledge about few web parts that you can use in your organization, to display formatted data using views to make it more presentable. You can retrieve data from an external source and display it to users without worrying about authoring the content or managing the same. You can define a plan of actions based on the tasks assigned to you and hence can manage your schedule more efficiently. You can collaborate with people and engage them with the help of Blogs/Discussions to make it more interactive. You should also better understand the power of web parts to configure it as per your requirements without writing any code.

Develop It Yourself – Exercises 2.0

Scenario: Your manager finds it difficult to track project tasks which are delayed. You need to propose a solution to display all those tasks that are running behind the schedule, in progress and 100% completed.

1. Create a Task list in team site
2. Create three views for task list (delayed, in progress and completed)
3. Apply respective filters on each view as per the requirement.
4. Create a page to display task details
5. Add required views on the page to display task details.

To get step-by-step instructions of exercises 2.0, visit our site.

DIY

In this section, we will cover, how to search content within SharePoint site using Content Search Web Part. In the later part of the section, we will cover, how to search an external source using federated search.

CONTENT SEARCH WEB PART

Microsoft introduced Content Search Web Part (CSWP) with SharePoint 2013 and it's available in SharePoint 2016 as well. In general, it provides the same functionalities as Content Query Web Part (CQWP).

Content Search Web Part allows you to query and display information from any site collection and beyond. Essentially, each Content Search Web Part is associated with a search query and shows the results for that search query.

Content Query Web Part uses various styling options to display dynamic content on SharePoint pages. In simpler words, you can use display templates to change, how search results appear on the page.

In this section, I'll walk you through two scenarios to display search results. In the first scenario, we will use Content Search Web Part, followed by Search Results Web Part for the second scenario. This is just to give a high-level idea about the usage of Content Search Web Part in a real-world scenario.

Scenario 1: Display data from a specific content type (Asset Library)

Asset Library: SharePoint's built-in Asset Library app is pre-configured to help you manage rich media assets, such as image, audio, and video files.

Asset Libraries feature:

- Thumbnail–centric views
- Overlay callouts
- Digital asset content types
- Automatic metadata extraction for image files

To achieve this functionality, let's create a new Asset Library called "Digital Assets"

1. Click Site icon and click "Add an app"
2. Type "asset" in search box and results will show "Asset Library" icon

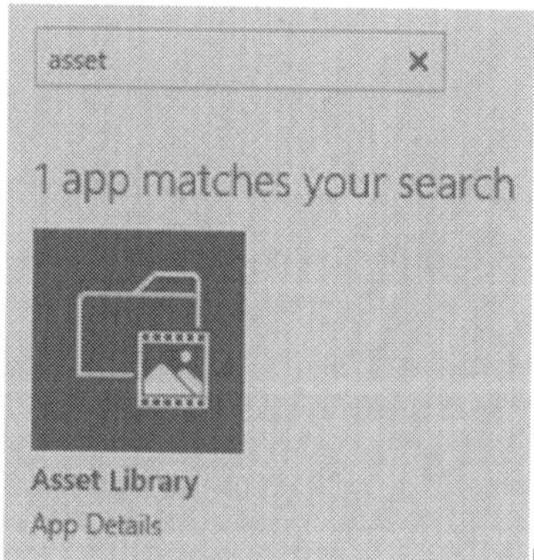

Figure 3.1 Asset Library Template

3. Click "Asset Library" and set the name for a new app to "Digital Assets".

Figure 3.2 Set Asset Library Name

4. Click **Create**

You just created a new Asset Library to store images, Audio and Video files. For this example, we will create items to store only videos (embed links).

Going forward, let's create couple of items for this library (**Content Type = Video**)

Title	**Description**	**Embed code**
SharePoint Server 2016	SharePoint 2016 extends innovation in Office 365 to your data center. Forged in the cloud, it's a whole new way to think about SharePoint.	<iframe width="560" height="315" src="https://www.youtube.com/embed/8gEzXfu6Wao" frameborder="0" allowfullscreen></iframe>
What's New in SharePoint 2016	Discuss the evolution of SharePoint, the new features found in SharePoint 2016, and the three biggest changes for admins who use SharePoint 2016.	<iframe width="560" height="315" src="https://www.youtube.com/embed/dDrQ3MFFmbc" frameborder="0" allowfullscreen></iframe>

After adding these two records, we will try to fetch these records using Content Search Web Part.

In this section, I'll walk you through, how to add the Content Search Web Part to your SharePoint site, as well as, how to configure the Web Part and display data based on the query.

1. Edit the page (Settings → Edit page)
2. Click "Add a Web Part" from any content zone where you want to show this web part
3. Under "Content Rollup" category, select **Content Search** Web Part
4. Click **Add** button
5. Select Content Search Web Part and "Edit Web Part" using web part properties.
6. In **Properties** section, under Search Criteria, click **Change Query** button
7. A new popup window will open, set the following properties
   a. Select a Query: Items matching a content type (system)
   b. Restrict by app: Current site collection
   c. Restrict by tag: Don't restrict by any tag
   d. Restrict by content type: Video

Note By default, all content types are not shown, so you need to select "--Show all Content Types--" to load all content types

Restrict by content type
You can limit results to a particular content type and all those that inherit from it.

Do not restrict on content type
Article Page
Audio
Document Set
Enterprise Wiki Page
Page
Report
Task
--Show all content types--

Figure 3.3 Select Content Type

8. Click OK

You should be able to see two results in Search Results preview

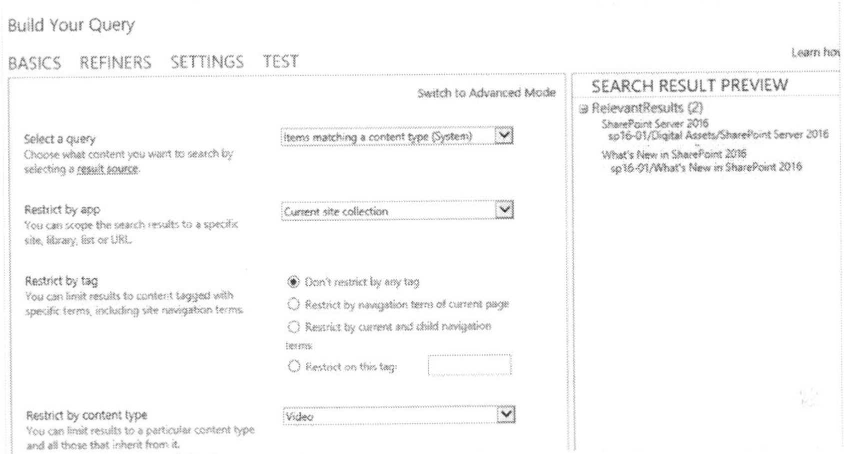

Figure 3.4 Search Results Preview

Set other properties as mentioned below.

1. Number of items to show: 2
2. In Display Template Section
   a. Control: List with Paging
   b. Item: Two lines

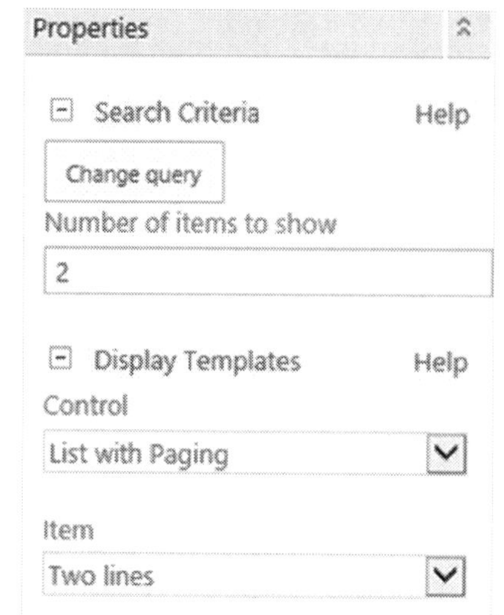

Figure 3.5 Content Search properties

3. In Property Mapping section
   a. Check "Change the mapping of managed properties for the fields in the Item Display Template."
   b. Link URL: Path
   c. Line 1: Title
   d. Line 2: Description

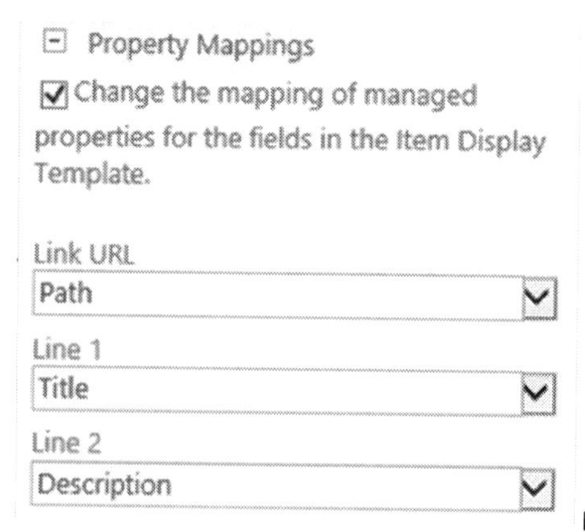

Figure 3.6 Property Mappings

4. In Appearance section
   a. Title: Content Search – Asset
   b. Chrome Type: Title and Border

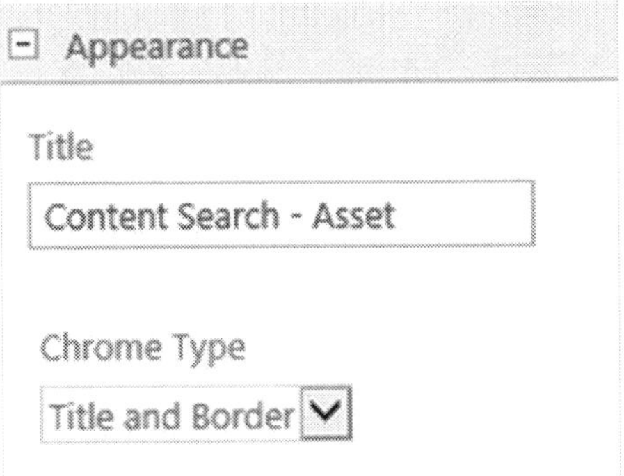

Figure 3.7 Content Search Appearance

5. Click OK

Content Search - Asset

SharePoint Server 2016
SharePoint 2016 extends innovation in Office 365 to your data center. Forged in the cloud, it's a whole new way t...

What's New in SharePoint 2016
Discuss the evolution of Sharepoint, the new features found in SharePoint 2016, and the three biggest changes f...

Figure 3.8 Content Search Results Output

Here we go!!! Using Content Search Web Part, we displayed our assets using custom query and changed the layout with display templates.

In our next section, we will try to achieve a spectacular functionality using Search Results Web Part. Are you ready?

FEDERATED SEARCH

SharePoint introduced a very cool feature to search external sources and display the searched results along with local SharePoint search results.

Importantly, external search results are not crawled by the SharePoint search server and return the results on demand.

In this example, we will set up a search to return content by BING search. SharePoint will format and display BING results along with results fetched from SharePoint local search. We can also display the results within a separate Web Part.

To achieve the above functionality we need to follow these steps

1. Create a new Result Source
2. Create new Query Rule
3. Add Search Results Web Part on the page
4. Configure Search Results Web Part
5. Add a Search Box Web Part
6. Configure Search Box Web Part to pass value to Search Results

Result Source: We can term it as containers for search results that hold results from specific sources and/or are filtered by specific criteria.

Create a new Federated Results Source for BING

1. Click **Settings** icon and click **Site Settings**
2. Under Search section, click **Result Sources**
3. Click **New Result Source**

4. Set following properties
   a. Name: Federated Results – Bing
   b. Description: Result source for Bing

c. Protocol: OpenSearch 1.0/1.1
d. Source Url: http://www.bing.com/search?q={?searchTerms}&format=rss&Market=en-Us
e. Credentials Information: Anonymous: This source does not require authentication

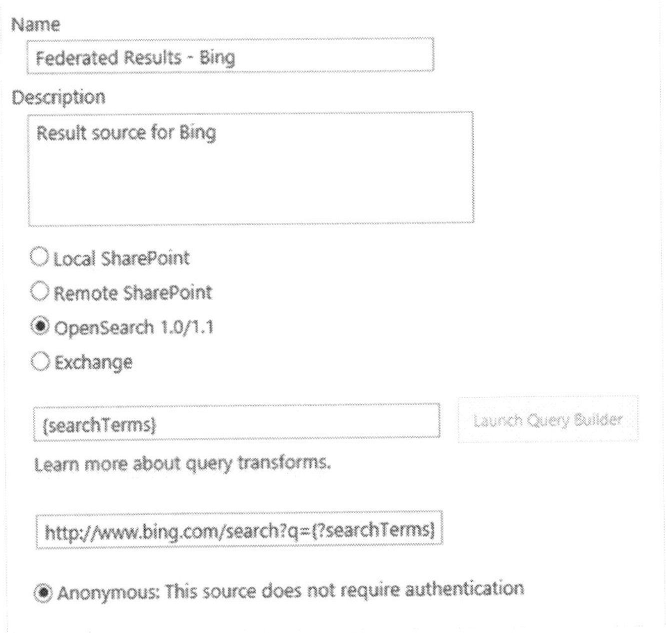

Figure 3.9 New Result Source Form

5. Click Save

Create a new Query Rule

1. Click **Settings** icon and click **Site Settings**
2. Under Search section, click **Query Rules**
3. Click **New Result Source**
4. Click down arrow, next to Select a Result Source... and then click Local SharePoint Results.

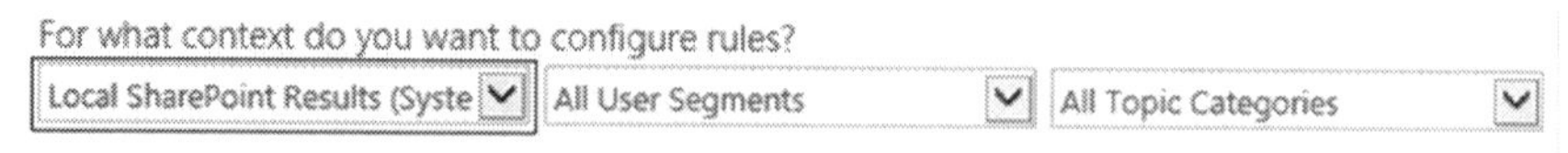

Figure 3.10 Result Source Properties

5. Click New Query Rule

   New Query Rule

6. Set the following properties in configuration

   a. Rule name: Bing Results

   b. In Query Conditions area, click **Remove Condition**

   c. In Actions area, click **Add Result Block** under Result Blocks

7. A popup window will open. Set the following properties for result block.

   a. In Blog Title section, Title: Bing Results for "{subjectTerms}"

   b. In Query section, Search this source, select "Federated Search – Bing" from the drop-down list.

   c. Click Settings to expand

      i. Check radio button "This block is always shown above core results"

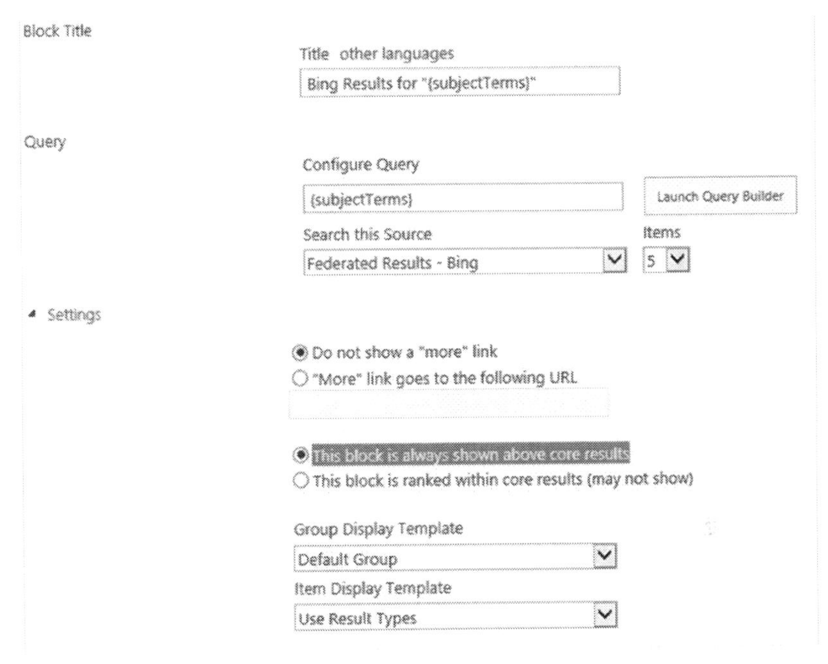

Figure 3.11 Result Block Configuration

ii. Click OK to close this popup window

8. Click Save to save this query rule

Add Search Results on a page

1. Go to the page where you want to display the search results
2. Click on site icon and click **Edit Page**
3. Click "Add a Web Part" where you want to display results. This example uses Header zone.
4. Under Search category, select **Search Results** Web Part and click Add button.

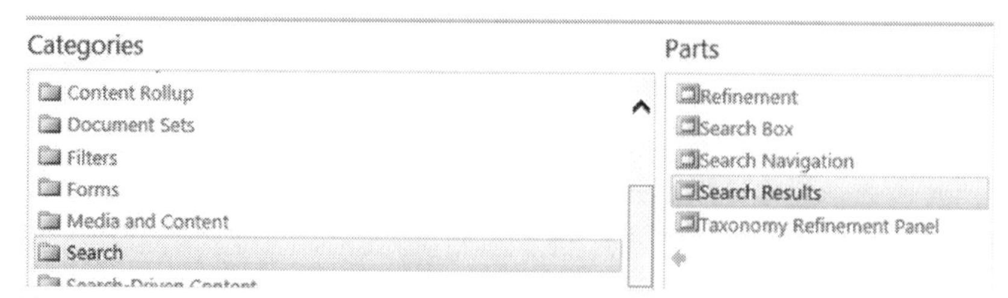

Figure 3.12 Search → Search Results

Configure Search Results Web Part

1. Select Search Results Web Part and Click "Edit Web Part"
2. In Properties for Search Results, under search Criteria, click "Change Query" button.
3. In Select a query section, make sure the item "Local SharePoint Results (System)" is selected. If not then select this from the drop-down list.

Figure 3.13 Select a Query

4. Click OK to save the changes.
5. Expand Settings, set Number of results per page to **3**

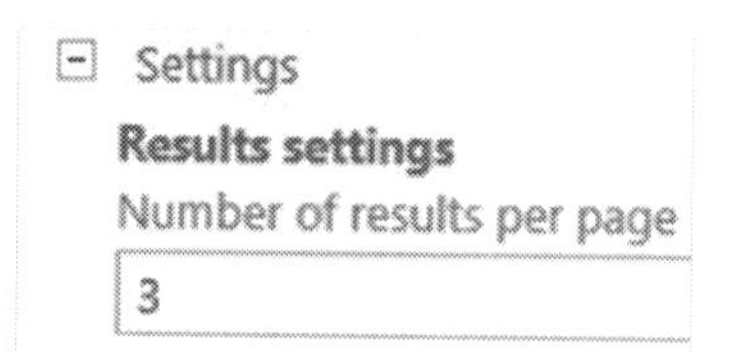

Figure 3.14 Results Settings

6. Expand Appearance, set Title to **Local - Search Results**
7. Set Chrome Type to **None**

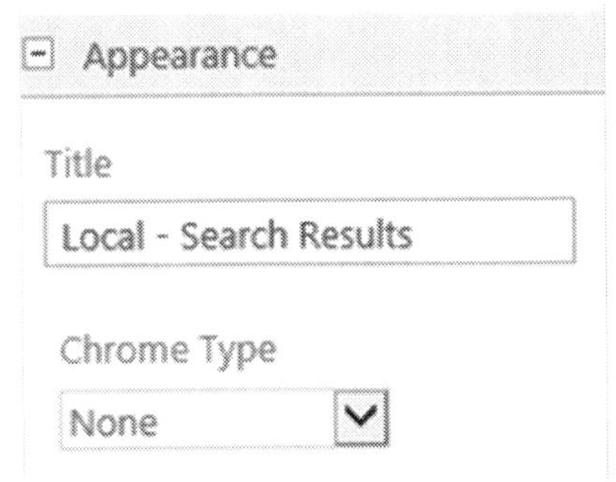

Figure 3.15 Content Search Appearance

8. Click **OK** to save the changes

Add Search Box Web Part on the page

1. Click site icon and click **Edit Page** (if not in edit mode)
2. Click "Add a Web Part"
3. Under Search category, select **Search Box** Web Part and click Add button.

Configure Search Results Web Part

1. Select Search Box Web Part and click "Edit Web Part"
2. Select "Send queries to other Web Parts on this page"
    a. Check "Local - Search Results"

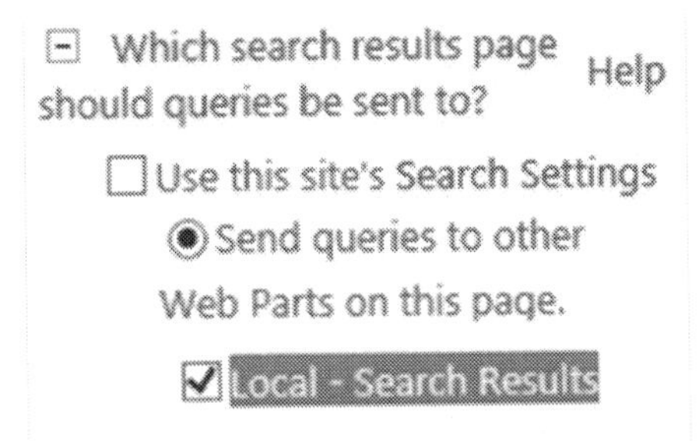

Figure 3.16 Select Result Source

    b. Click OK to save the changes

3. Save the Page

At moment, you cannot see any data and page will look like this,

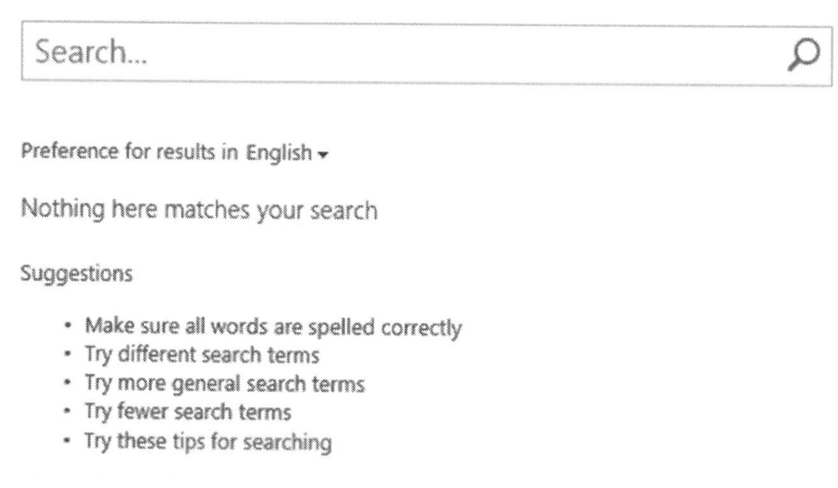

Figure 3.17 Search Box Web Part

Type "SharePoint" in Search Box and click search icon.... You can see that there are multiple records shown in Search Results web part.

There are two parts in search results based on the parameter typed and passed as search criteria.

Part 1: Results fetched via BING search and shown on top of the results.

Part 2: Results returned from our local SharePoint based on the above parameter.

Note

As we did not have any rule defined in our query hence it returned all matching records across all content types (i.e. documents, images, videos, etc.)

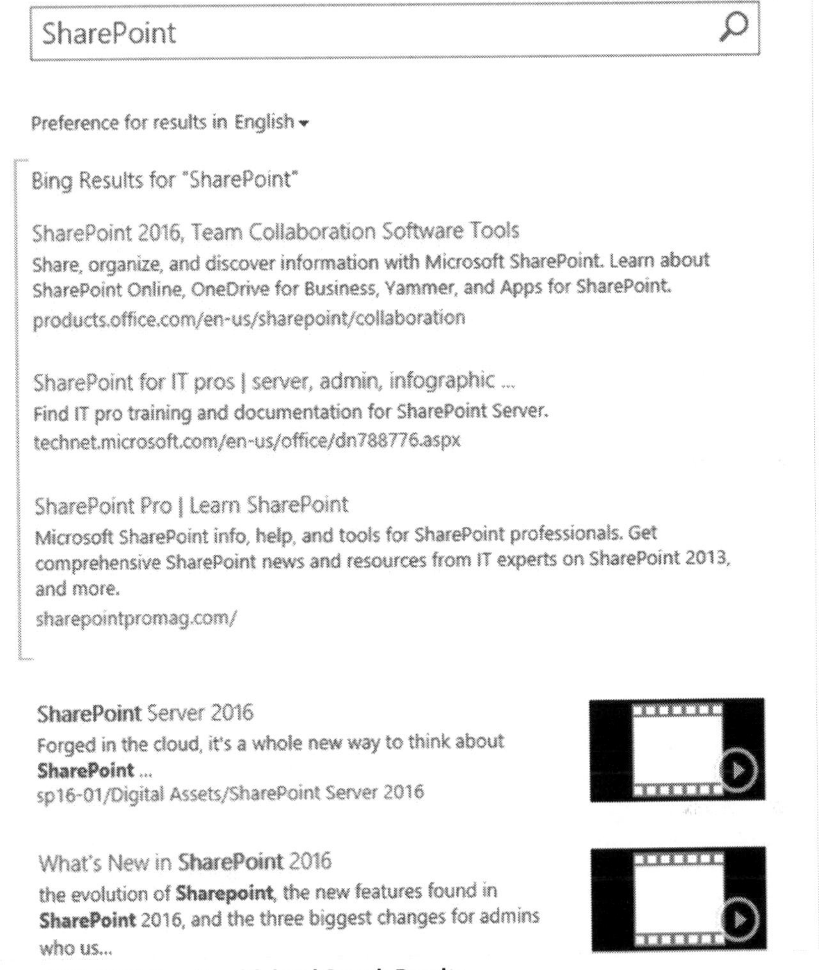

Figure 3.18 BING Results with local Search Results

As I mentioned earlier, this a great feature to display data from local SharePoint site as well as an external search engine without writing a single line of code. **Isn't that amazing!!!**

Summary:

This chapter provided a high-level knowledge to searching specific content types within SharePoint site. You should also understand the concept of searching content via external sources. This chapter also provided information to make data available easily for end users.

Develop It Yourself – Exercises 3.0

Scenario: You are working on a marketing campaign project along with other team members. Your team continuously works on a number of documents for that campaign. Your manager needs to keep a close eye on each document which was recently updated. You need to implement a feasible solution to display documents with a timestamp.

1. Create a document library in team site
2. Create additional columns to store other attributes
    a. Doc Type (Drop down list – Internal, Public, Customer)
    b. Editor (Person or Group)
    c. Status (Radio buttons – Active / Inactive)
3. Create a page to display document listing
4. Use Content Search Web Part to the page
5. Configure Content Search Web Part to get desired results

To get step-by-step instructions of exercises 3.0, visit our site.

DIY

CONTENT TYPES

The content type is an essential building block in SharePoint. It can be defined as a set of columns that are grouped together to serve a specific purpose. For example, you can create a content type (a group of columns) called "Product" using which you'll be able to insert items in a list or library to store product information.

As per Microsoft definition

"A content type is a reusable collection of metadata (columns), workflow, behaviour, and other settings for a category of items or documents in a SharePoint list or document library. Content types enable you to manage the settings for a category of information in a centralized, reusable way".

In general, there is a perception that reusability is the biggest advantage for using content type. However, in a real-world scenario, content types provide a way more than just reusability characteristic (columns, workflow). One of the features of content type is to create custom document template adhering to your organization templates.

Another important feature is that you can use many content types inside a list/library. This way you can have a different set of columns for different items or documents within the same list or library.

By looking at the definition, some users find it simple to understand content types but the majority of the users tend to get confused as they proceed. **But don't worry!!!**

In this section, I'll walk you through creating a content type to add and manage product information. In this example, we will create a content type for the product. To proceed further, you first need to define the basic schema for Product list.

Column Name	Data Type
Title	Text
Product ID	Text
Product Description	Multi-text
IsActive	Boolean

As we know content type is a collection of columns so we need to create the columns first.

Create site columns

1. Go to **Site settings** using Site settings icon
2. Under Web Designer Galleries, click Site columns
3. Click Create icon located on top
4. Set the following properties

Name	Attributes
Product ID	Column name: Product ID Type: Single line of text Group: Select New Group and enter "Product Columns"

5. Click OK
6. Create following columns via clicking on Create icon

Note

We do not need to create group again and can be selected from existing group drop down menu

7. Set the following properties

Name	Attributes
Product Description	Column name: Product Description Type: Multiple lines of text Group: Select "Product Columns" from Existing Group
IsActive	Column name: IsActive Type: Yes/No (Check box) Group: Select "Product Columns" from Existing Group

Post creating all required columns, you can select "Product Columns" from Show Group to filter our columns.

Figure 4.1 Site Columns Listing

Next step is to create content type, let's begin

Create content type

1. Go to **Site settings** using Site settings icon
2. Under Web Designer Galleries, click Site content types
3. Click Create icon located on top
4. Set the following properties
   a. Name: Product
   b. Description: Product related info
   c. Select parent content type from: List Content Types

   d. Parent Content Type: Item
   e. Group: Select New Group and enter "Product Content Types"
5. Click OK to save the changes

It will take you to Product site content type information page

Site Content Types › Site Content Type

Site Content Type Information
Name: Product
Description: Product related info
Parent: Item
Group: Product Content Types

Settings

- Name, description, and group
- Advanced settings
- Workflow settings
- Delete this site content type
- Information management policy settings
- Manage document conversion for this content type

Columns

Name	Type
Title	Single line of text

- Add from existing site columns
- Add from new site column
- Column order

Figure 4.2 List's Content Type Information Page

Click "Add from existing site columns"

Note

If you realize, we did not include "Title" column in our schema. We can use Title column from Item content type.

Add following properties to add previously created columns and click OK.

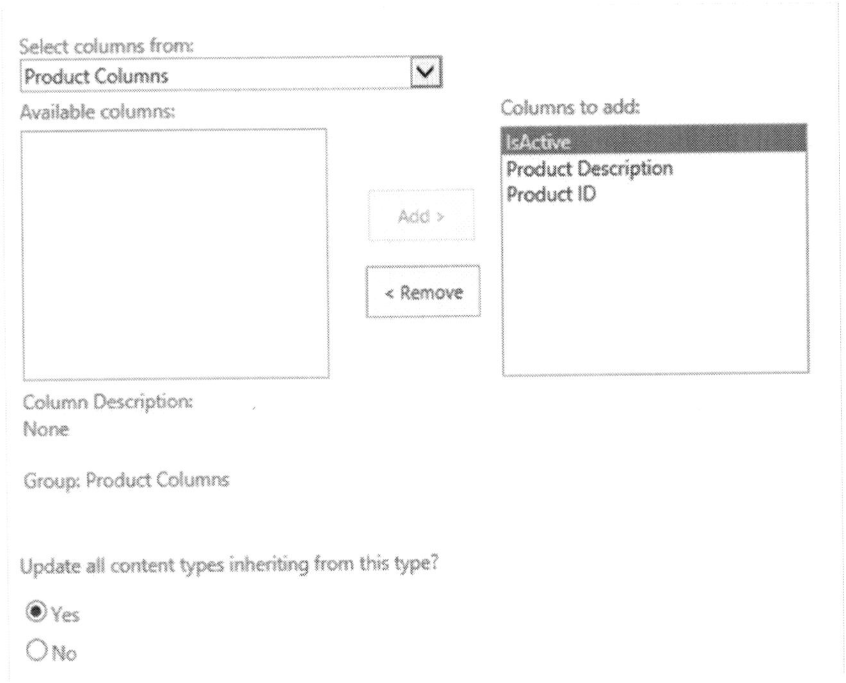

Select columns from:
Product Columns
Available columns:
Columns to add:
IsActive
Product Description
Product ID
Add >
< Remove
Column Description:
None
Group: Product Columns
Update all content types inheriting from this type?
Yes
No

Figure 4.3 Adding Site Columns to Content Type

You have successfully added all site columns to Product content type.

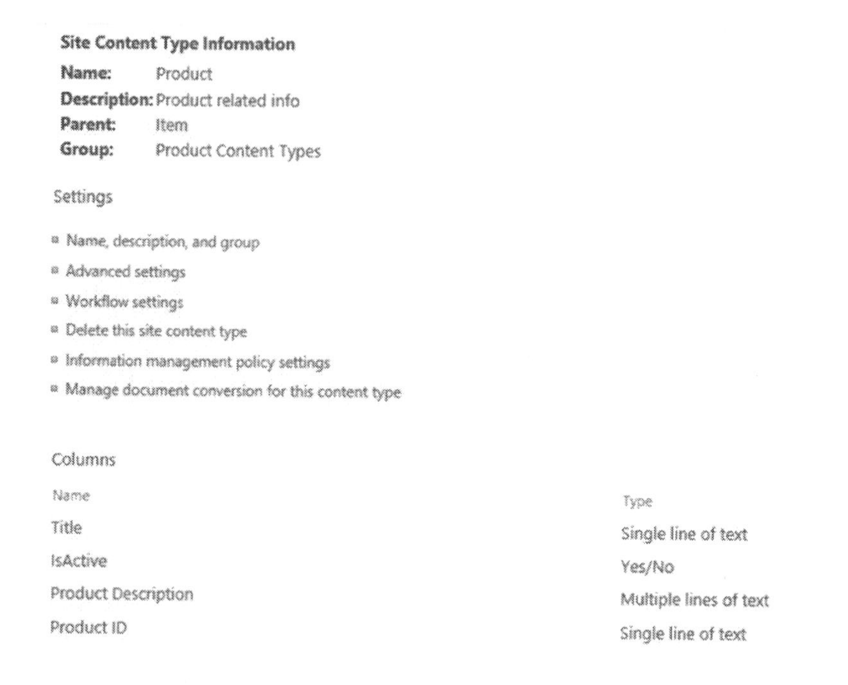

Figure 4.4 Site Content Type Information Page

Next step is to create a custom list and include Product content type to that list. This way you can include all these columns to the newly created list.

1. Click **Add an app** using Site settings icon
2. Click Custom List icon and set name "Product Info"

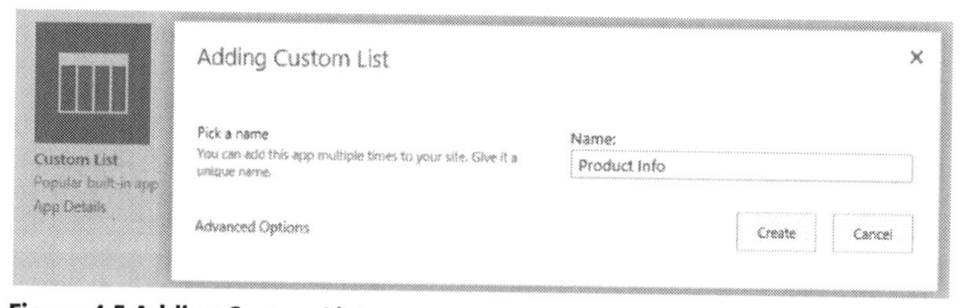

Figure 4.5 Adding Custom List

3. Click Create button

Apply content type

1. Click "Product Info" icon and select "Settings" from popup menu

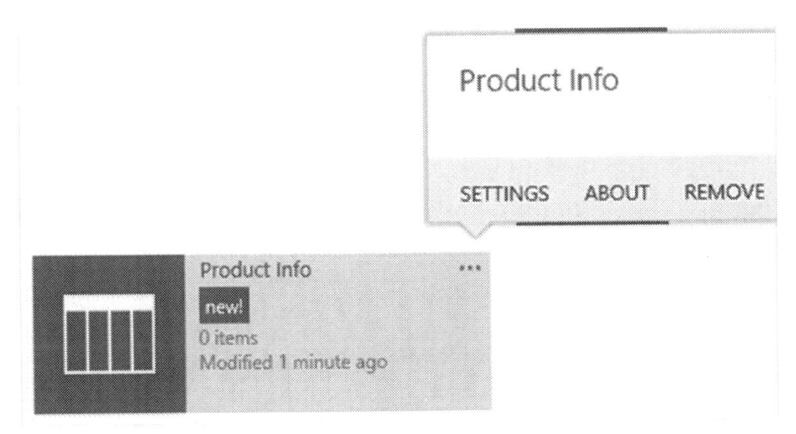

Figure 4.6 List Eclipse (...) Menu

2. From Product Info setting page, under General settings, click Advanced settings
3. Set "Allow management of content types?" to Yes
4. Click OK

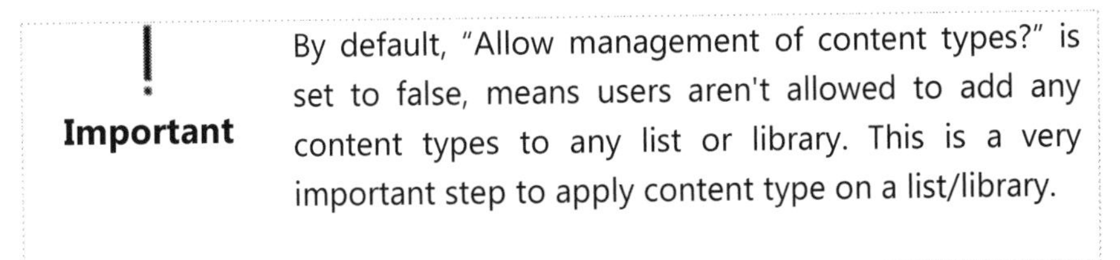

Important

By default, "Allow management of content types?" is set to false, means users aren't allowed to add any content types to any list or library. This is a very important step to apply content type on a list/library.

6. Under Content types section, click "Add from existing site content types"
7. In column, Select site content types from: select "Product Content Types"
8. Select Product and move to right hand-side section
9. Click OK

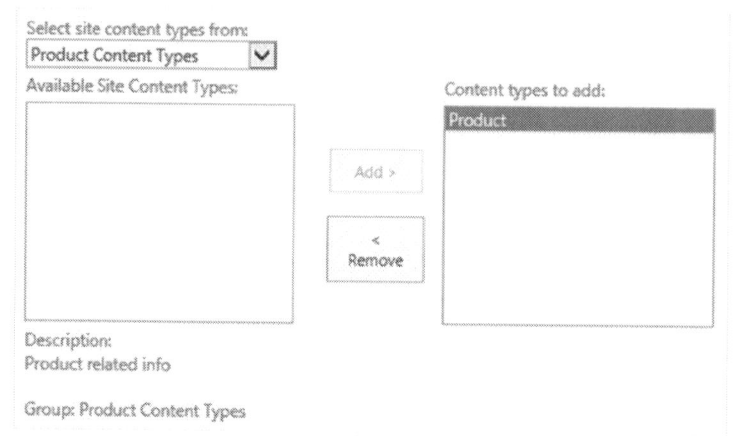

Figure 4.7 Adding Columns to Content Type

As you can see, Product Info list is inheriting columns from two content types i.e. Item and Product.

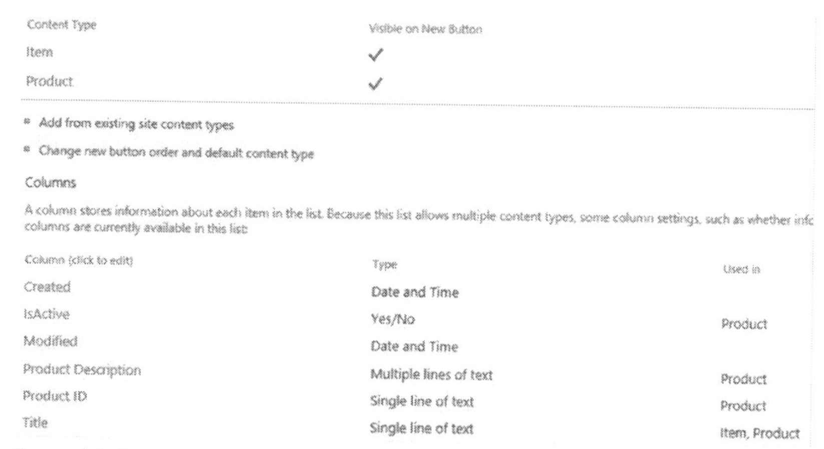

Figure 4.8 List Setting Information about Content Types

We are now ready to use Product Info list to store information.

Go to Product Info list which would be empty so far.

Once you click on ITEMS tab from top ribbon and click New Item down arrow link, you can see there are two types of items available.

1. Item
2. Product

Figure 4.9 New Content Type

Note

This is just to demonstrate, how to include multiple content types in a list/library. Let's get rid of item type.

1. Go to "Product Info" List Settings

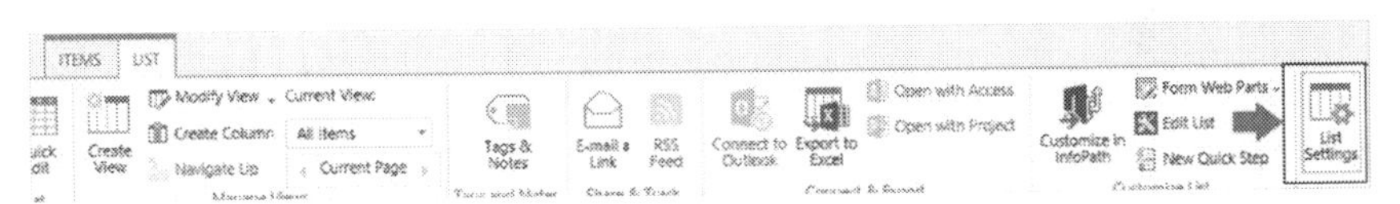

Figure 4.10 List Setting Icon

2. Under Content types section, click "Change new button order and default content type"
3. Uncheck "Visible" for Item and set "Position from Top" to 1 for Product Info

Visible	Content Type	Position from Top
☐	Item	2
☑	Product	1

Figure 4.11 Content Type Visibility and Ordering

4. Click OK

Figure 4.12 New Product Content Type

You can only add Product type item to this list. Let's add a new Product Info.

Click New Item followed by Product.

Figure 4.13 New Product Form

Oh! Something is OFF, isn't it? Yes, the column orders. Let's fix it quickly.

1. Go to Product info list settings

2. Under content Types, click Product
3. Under Columns, click Column order

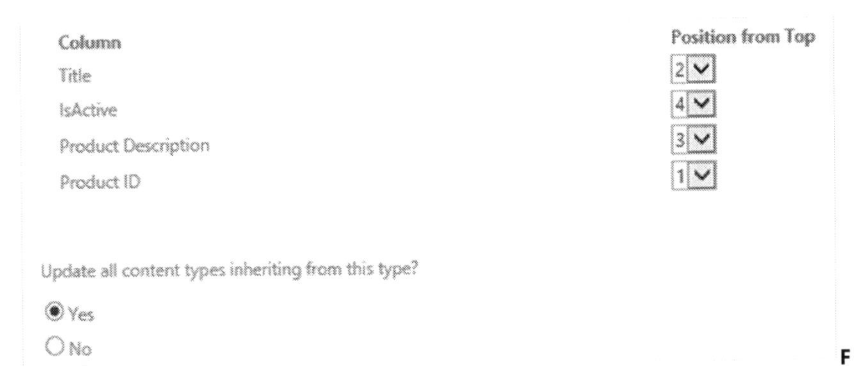

Figure 4.14 List Columns Ordering

4. Set the column sequence and click OK
5. Go back to list and click new Product

Product Info

Product ID

Title *

Product Description

IsActive

Save Cancel

Figure 4.15 Updated Column Ordering In Product Form

Much better now!!!!

You can add few products and it may look like this.

Product Info

✓	Product ID	Title	Product Description	IsActive
	PROD-01	Product 1	Product 1 description	Yes
	PROD-02	Product 2	Product 2 description	Yes
	PROD-03	Product 3	Product is no longer in use	No

Figure 4.16 Product Info List View

Splendid!!!! You are absolutely ready to use, create and appreciate the power of content types.

You can achieve a lot more using Content types such as associating a workflow or define document template if using Document Library.

Before I conclude, here's my two cents... You need to be very careful while choosing the Parent of content type. In our case, we selected Item as Parent for Product Content Type and applied on the custom list (Item).

The point to drive home is that parent type of Content Type and parent of list / library should be same. Otherwise, it will not work if you choose the wrong parent...

MANAGED METADATA

In general, Metadata can be defined as information about information. Information could be anything such as Product category, Author, place, department, etc.

In SharePoint, we can create and manage metadata centrally, which helps,

1. To standardize documentation
2. To easily find documents / items based on metadata
3. Number of people uploading and accessing the files

In the modern world, with the help of metadata, we can discourage users to create folders, instead, they can tag documents using metadata.

In this section, we will look at the definitions of some key terminology that are associated to "Managed Metadata".

Taxonomy:

A taxonomy is a hierarchical classification of related words, labels or terms that are organized into logical groups. For example, you can create a hierarchical information about Departments in an organization e.g.

Department

a. Finance
b. Human Resource
c. Information technology
d. Marketing

Folksonomy:

A folksonomy can be termed as a classification system using which users can collaborate on words, labels, and terms on a site. A folksonomy-based approach to metadata can be useful to share the knowledge and expertise of site users. By using a folksonomy, content classification can evolve together with changing business needs and user interests.

Term Set:

A Term set is a group of related terms. Terms sets can be restricted by defining its scope based on where it is created. A term set can be defined as local or global.

Local term sets are created within the context of a site collection and are available for use (and visible) only to users of that site collection.

Global term sets are available for use, across all sites that subscribe to a specific Managed Metadata Service application.

Term sets can be configured as closed, means users cannot add new terms to the term set, whereas if configured as open Term sets then users can add new terms to the term set.

Terms:

A term is a single item within a term set. It's a specific word or phrase that you associated with an item on a SharePoint site. A term has a unique ID that can have many text labels (synonyms). If you need to define a term set for a multilingual site then the term can have labels in different languages.

There are two types of terms:

- *Managed terms* are terms that are pre-defined and Term Store administrators or other users having the same rights organize managed terms into a hierarchical term set.

- *Enterprise keywords – An enterprise keyword* can be defined as a word or phrase that a user adds to items on a SharePoint site. The collection of enterprise keywords is known as the Keywords set. Typically, users can add any word or phrase to an item as a keyword. This means that you can use enterprise keywords for folksonomy-style tagging. Sometimes, Term Store administrators move enterprise keywords into a specific managed term set. When they are part of a managed term set, keywords become available in the context of that term set.

Group:

Using groups you can apply security boundaries. A group is a set of term sets that all share common security requirements. Only those users who are designated as contributors to a specific group can manage term sets that belong to the group or create new term sets within it. Organizations should create unique groups for term sets that will have unique access or security needs.

Term Store Management Tool:

The Term Store Management Tool is the tool that people who manage taxonomies use to create or manage term sets and the terms within them. The Term Store Management tool displays all the global term sets and any local term sets available for the site collection from which you access the Term Store Management Tool.

Managed Metadata column:

A Managed Metadata column is a special kind of column that you can add to lists or libraries. It enables site users to select terms from a specific term set. A Managed Metadata column can map to an existing term set, or you can create a local term set specifically for the column.

Enterprise Keywords column:

The enterprise Keywords column is a column that you can add to content types, lists, or libraries to enable users to tag items with words or phrases that they choose. By default, it is a multi-value column. When users type a word or phrase into the column, SharePoint presents type-ahead suggestions. Type-ahead suggestions might include items from managed term sets and the Keywords term set. Users can select an existing value, or enter something new.

METADATA EXAMPLES

In this section, I'll walk you through the feature of Managed Navigation. Using Managed Navigation you can design a site navigation that is driven by terms or topics rather than (site) structure.

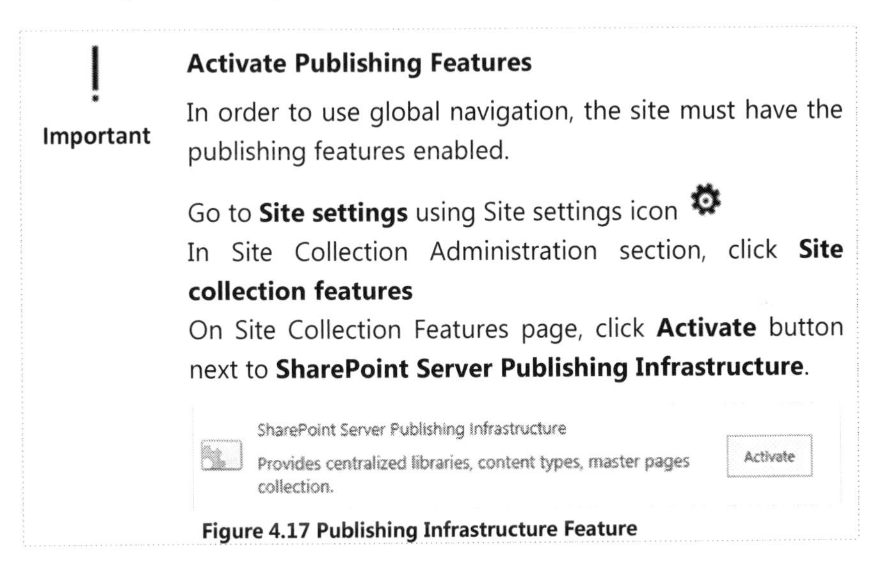

Important

Activate Publishing Features

In order to use global navigation, the site must have the publishing features enabled.

Go to **Site settings** using Site settings icon
In Site Collection Administration section, click **Site collection features**
On Site Collection Features page, click **Activate** button next to **SharePoint Server Publishing Infrastructure**.

Figure 4.17 Publishing Infrastructure Feature

Enable Managed Navigation

1. Go to **Site settings** using Site settings icon
2. Under Look and Feel section, click **Navigation**
3. Select Managed Navigation for both the sections i.e. Global and Current Navigation

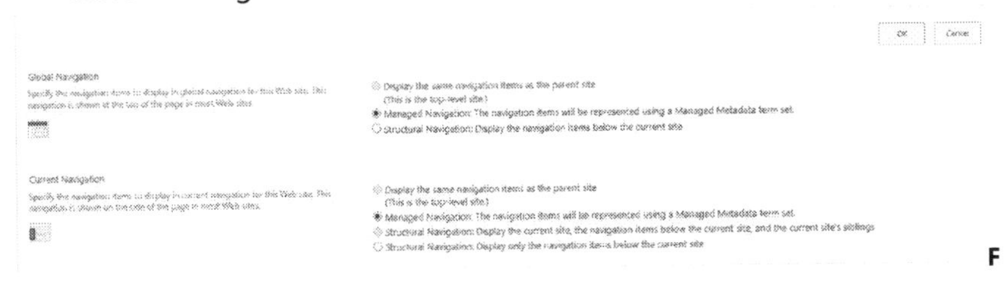

F

igure 4.18 Site Navigation Options

4. Click OK button to save the changes.

When managed navigation is enabled, you can easily manage terms using the Term Store Management Tool. A new term set is created within the site collection Term Store to host all terms associated with the navigation.

Edit Navigation

Let's create a simple navigation structure consisting of three items i.e. Home, News and How To. We can create News as a sub item for Home.

1. Go to **Site settings** using Site settings icon
2. Under Site Administration, click **Term store management**
3. In left section, expand Managed Metadata Service (if collapsed)
4. Expand **Site Collection** element
5. Select **Site Navigation** element

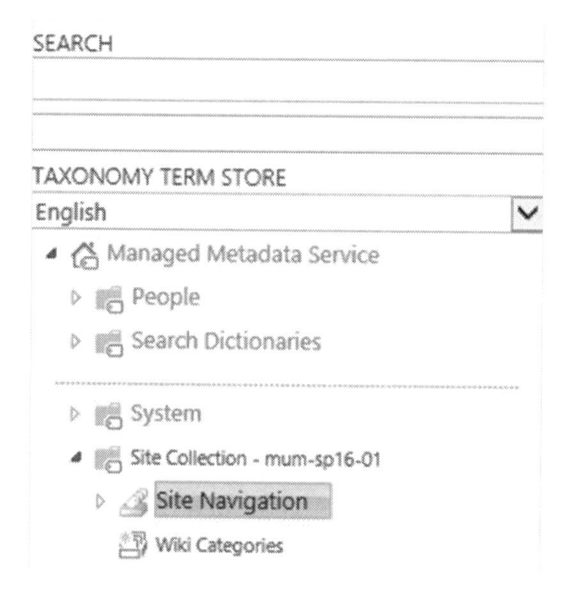

Figure 4.19 Term Store Management

6. Right-click on Site Navigation and click **Create Term**

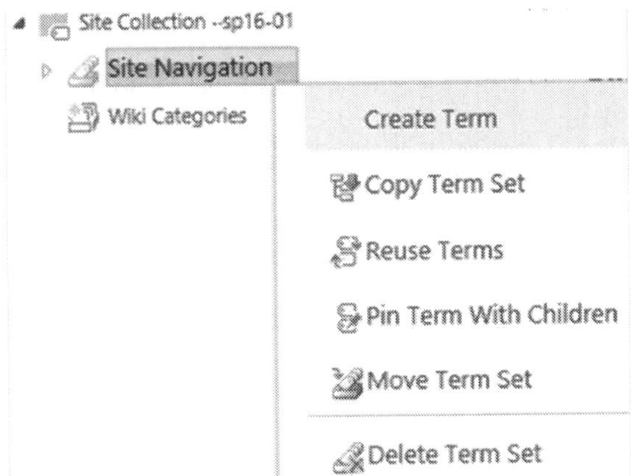

Figure 4.20 Create Term

7. Type "Home" to newly created item
8. In right side section, in General tab set Default Label: Home

Figure 4.21 Term Properties

9. Select Navigation tab. Under Navigation Node Type, select Simple Link or Header
10. Click Browser button
11. From left side section select site pages and from right side select Home.aspx

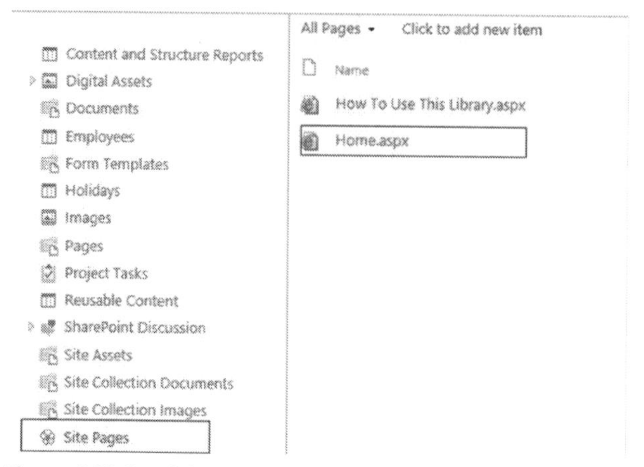

Figure 4.22 Set Link Or Header

12. Click Insert button
13. Click Save button to save the changes
14. Repeat the steps 6-13 to create another item for How To

You need to select "How To Use This Library.aspx"

Note

In this example, I used news.aspx page (created previously) in pages. I would recommend you to create News.aspx and store in Pages folder.

In order to create a sub-menu, you need to select HOME as a parent. Repeat the steps 6 to 13 to create News menu. The final layout will look like as shown in next image.

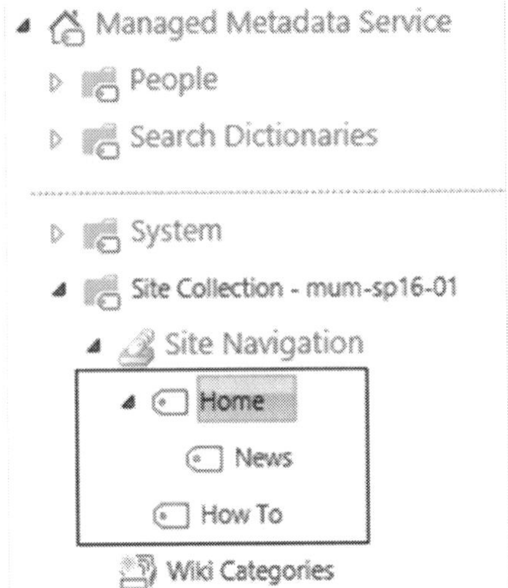

Figure 4.23 Set Menu Options

Now, you can navigate to our home page to verify the changes.

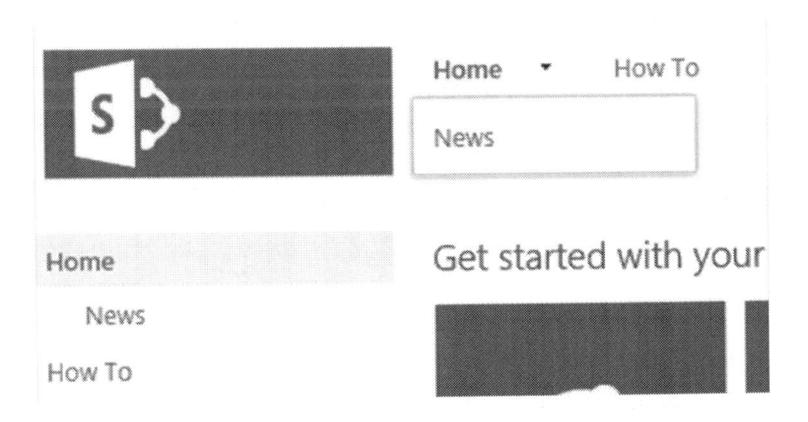

Figure 4.24 Custom Navigation Menu

Now you have newly created a menu on top of the page as well as left side section.

Great!!! We just learned how to configure managed navigation and it's up to you to use this feature to implement great navigation functionalities without any prior experience.

Summary:

This chapter provided basic knowledge about the governance in SharePoint. You should understand the concept of categorizing your documents to make it search friendly and to manage more efficiently. This chapter also provided sufficient knowledge to create a hierarchal structure using metadata and its uses.

Develop It Yourself – Exercises 4.0

Scenario: You need to manage various in-house products for your organization. Most of the users complain that it is very difficult to find products easily. You also need to provision a better way to assign predefined tags to products.

1. Create term sets needed for product keywords
2. Create a site column to store product keywords
3. Create a Base Product document content type based on the document parent content type and place it in a group. [**Hint:** you can follow the same steps mentioned above to create Product Item content type, make sure you select Document instead of item]
4. Create a Products document library using newly created content type
5. Add products documents to this library.

To get step-by-step instructions of exercises 4.0, visit our site.

DIY

NAVIGATION IN SHAREPOINT

There are times when you visit a SharePoint Site, feel lost and get confused where to click or start? In this section, I'll talk about SharePoint Navigation. BTW, we just covered Managed Navigation in the previous section.

A thoughtful and smartly implemented navigation, helps users to find desired contents quickly and that becomes a key aspect of User Adoption.

Navigation types

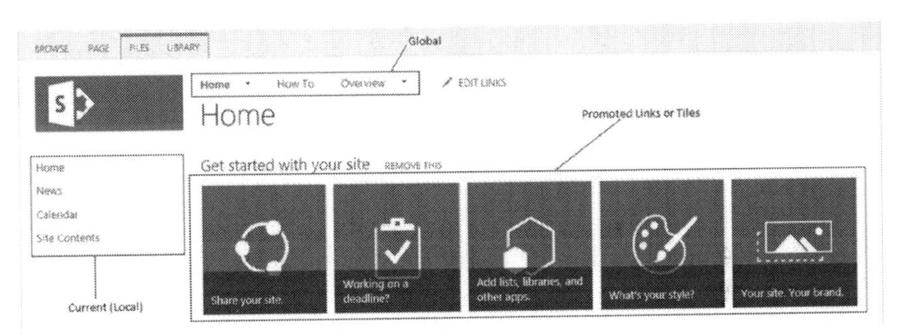

Figure 5.1 Navigation Types in SharePoint 2016

Global SharePoint Navigation

It is meant for "global" site navigation. In our previous section, we created Home, News and How To links that appeared on top of the page (horizontal menu)

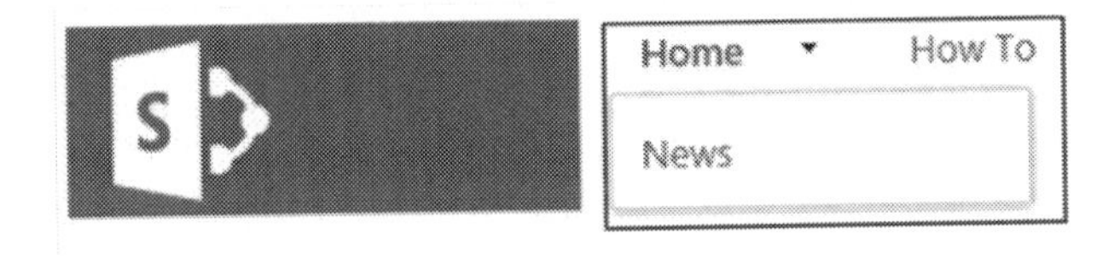

Figure 5.2 Custom Horizontal Menu

There are two options to implement global navigation i.e. Structural Navigation or Managed Navigation

As discussed in the previous section, Managed navigation items will be represented using a Managed Metadata term set.

Structural Navigation displays only navigation items for the current site. You can also set it to include subsites and pages in navigation.

Local SharePoint Navigation

This is commonly known as "Quick Launch" which appears on the left-hand side of page or site (Vertical). It also meant "local" or "current" navigation within a site.

Figure 5.3 Quick Launch

SharePoint Navigation via Promoted Links or SharePoint Tiles

Here, I'll talk about a very useful feature called "SharePoint Tiles" (also known as Promoted Links). It's an easy way to enhance your site navigation in a very user-friendly manner for end-users. Let's start implementing using easy steps.

In principal, Promoted Links web part is a list of graphic icons that you can link to URLs for quick and easy access.

1. Click **Add an app** using Site settings icon
2. Type "Promoted" in find an app search box
3. Choose Promoted Links Web Part

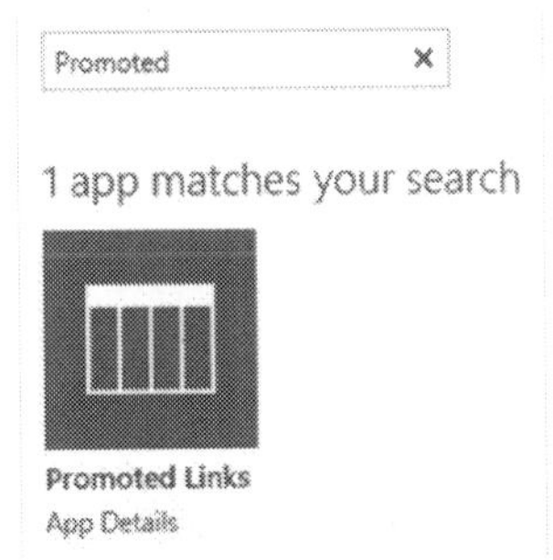

Figure 5.4 Promoted Links Template

4. Set Name to "Quick Link"
5. Go to Quick Link list and open it

Note

It will show the message that the list is empty.

Quick Link

The list is empty. Add tiles from the All Promoted Links view.

Figure 5.5 Empty List

6. Click "All Promoted Links" to configure SharePoint Tiles
7. Click new item to insert a new item
8. Set following properties for new item

   A. Title: Calendar

   Uses: This is the title of the icon, layered over the image/title.

B. Background Image Location: Pick any image from **local SharePoint environment**

Uses: I would recommend using .PNG (transparent) image having size 150 pixels X 150 pixels. Provide full qualified path of the image.

C. Description: (Optional) this appears when the user hovers over the icon. You can provide additional information about that item.

D. Link Location: Path URL for item

Uses: User will be taken to path URL once clicks on Icon. You can provide additional information in the description just below it (again optional).

E. Launch Behavior: In Page Navigation

Uses: It tells SharePoint, how URL will be opened. Keep it default.

F. Order: 1

Uses: It defines the sequence number for icons to display from left to right.

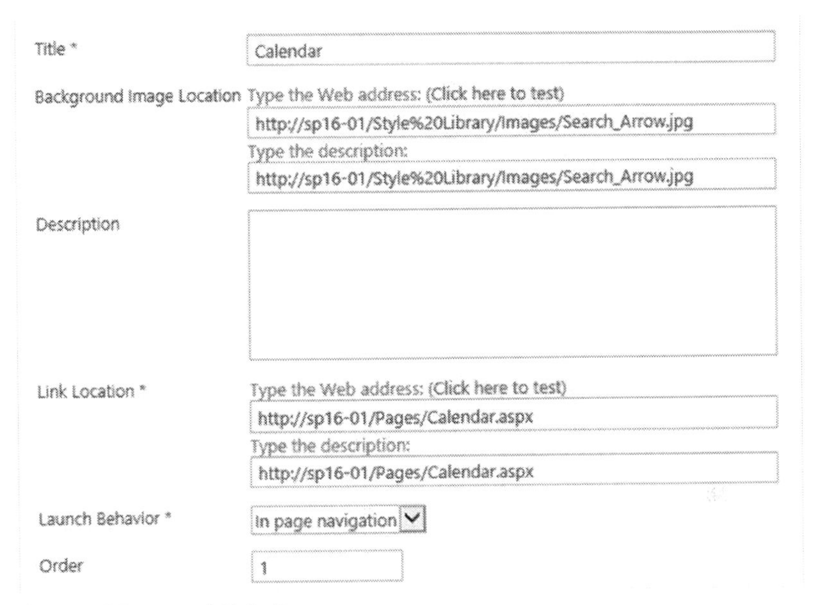

Figure 5.6 Promoted Links Form

9. Insert new items and follow all the steps described in point 8 (A to E). Your final output would look like this.

Title	Background Image Location	Description	Link Location	Launch Behavior	Order
Calendar	http://mum-sp16-01/Style%20Library/Images/Search_Arrow.jpg		http://mum-sp16-01/Pages/Calendar.aspx	In page navigation	1
News	http://mum-sp16-01/Style%20Library/Images/Search_Arrow_RTL.jpg		http://mum-sp16-01/Pages/News.aspx	In page navigation	2

Figure 5.7 List with Promoted Links Items

We are all set and done!!! Go to your homepage or any other page where you want to add this web part.

1. Edit the page
2. Click "Add a Web Part"
3. Under Apps category, select "Quick Link" and click Add button

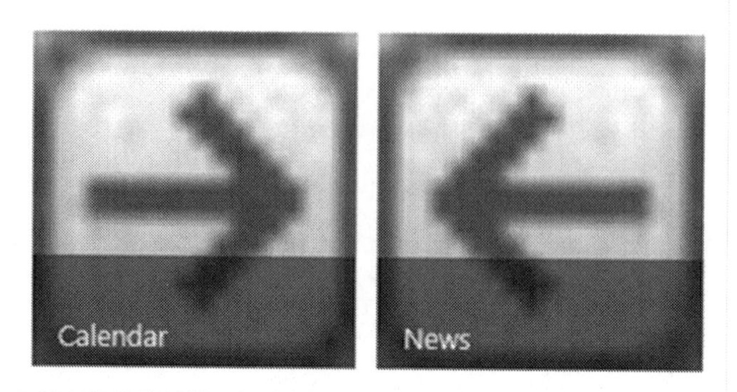

Figure 5.8 Promoted Links in Action

WOW!!! Promoted Links are a great way to provide quick access to various actions with just one click.

SHAREPOINT BRANDING

SharePoint branding is commonly defined as the colors, fonts, logos, and supporting graphics that make up the general look and feel of any website. In a nutshell, it is to applying organization branding to the SharePoint interface to make visually appealing and having a consistent layout.

You can apply Branding by changing the look and feel of your site through built-in template changes or more detailed and organizationally driven branding. Since Branding is quite an abstract word and hence there's no one straight answer. In this chapter, I'll demonstrate the Out-of-the-box configuration for the look and feel using master pages, themes, etc.

Themes:

Themes provide a quick and easy way to apply lightweight branding to a SharePoint site. Using themes, users (site owner, designer rights) can customize a site by changing the site layout, color palette, font scheme, and background image.

Theming experience includes following components to apply the brandings to your SharePoint sites. In this section, I'll be concentrating on SharePoint themes.

! Important	It is important to understand that Office 365 themes and SharePoint themes are different. It's also important to understand SharePoint themes and composed looks are used to brand SharePoint sites.

Color palette: A color scheme, which can be defined as a combination of colors that are used in a site. This is also referred to as SharePoint theme which is available in the design gallery. Color palettes are .spcolor (xml) files, stored in the Theme Gallery of the root site of the site collection.

Font scheme: A font scheme, defines the fonts that are used in a site. Font schemes are .spfont (xml) files, stored in the Theme Gallery of the root site of the site collection.

Background image: The background image that is used on the site.

Master page: A master page provides a single point of branding and structure that you can leverage across a SharePoint site.

SharePoint 2016 comes with preinstalled themes (also referred to as designs or composed looks). Either you can use preinstalled themes or create custom themes. In this section, I'll walk you through choosing a preinstalled theme for your publishing site.

1. Go to Home page of your publishing site (you can start with your root site collection)
2. Click **Site settings** using Site settings icon ⚙
3. Under Look and Feel section, click **Change the look**

You can select any theme from preinstalled themes.

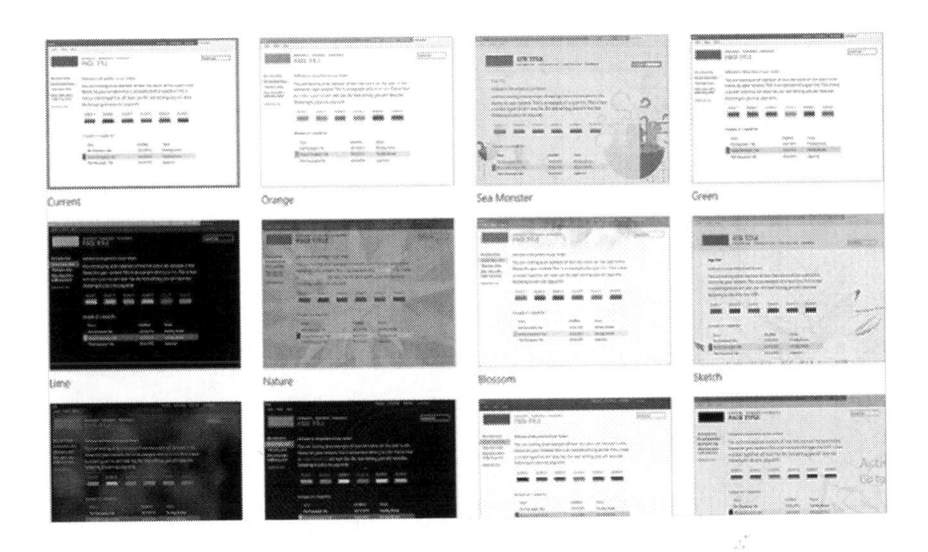

Figure 5.9 Themes Available In SharePoint 2016

4. Scroll down and select "Breeze" theme

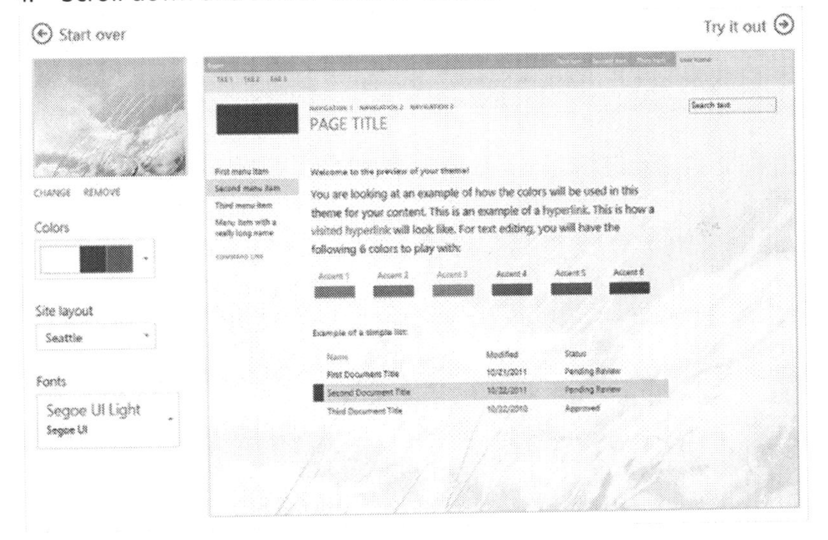

Figure 5.10 Theme Configuration Form

5. Change Color, layout, and Fonts as shown below (you can choose your favorite style)

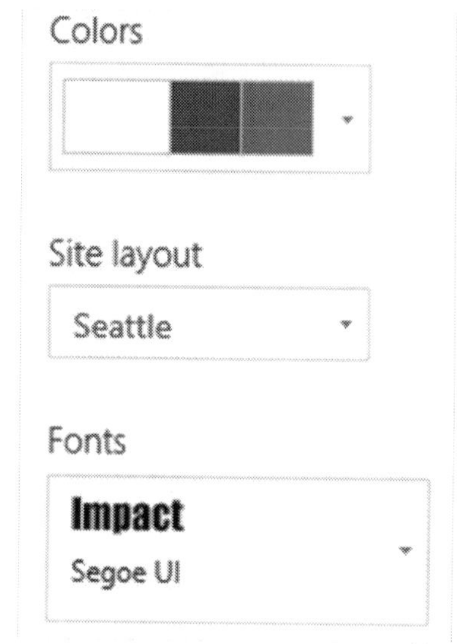

Figure 5.11 Change Color, Layout, and Fonts

6. Click **Try it out** to get a preview of your site with its new theme.

Note

Tip: If you like the look, click "Yes, keep it". This takes you to the Site Settings page where you can modify the title and logo or configure additional settings. If you don't like the theme, click "No, not quite there" and repeat steps 2 through 4.

7. For now, click **Yes, keep it**

Fantastic!!! You are now ready to flaunt your new design to woo SharePoint users.

Summary:

You should understand the techniques to implement navigation easily and quickly. This chapter also provided you the knowledge to play around with pre-defined themes to enhance the look and feel of your site.

Develop It Yourself – Exercises 5.0

Scenario: You need to provide a quick and easy access to in-house products. You are also planning to replace existing theme with a new one to make it more vibrant as well as having an airy feel.

1. Link your Product document library with quick links
2. Select new theme using pre-defined themes (try out font style, colors)

To get step-by-step instructions of exercises 5.0, visit our site.

DIY

SHAREPOINT LISTS FORMS

SharePoint lists and libraries contain list forms that allow users to display, edit, and add items to a list or library.

In a custom list form, you can show or hide certain fields, reorganize those fields, change the layout of the form, add formatted text and graphics, and ultimately, change the XSL, HTML, or ASP used by the form.

Note

You can only perform these tasks by creating a custom list form in SharePoint Designer 2013.

Using SharePoint Designer 2013, you can quickly create customized interfaces for SharePoint lists using forms. By default, there are three forms associated with a list i.e. DispForm.aspx, EditForm.aspx and NewForm.aspx.

1. DispForm – This is a display form to show single item details of a list or library in a read-only mode.

2. EditForm – On editing any existing record, the user can update attributes of selected item or document.

3. NewForm – Using this form, the user can add a new item to a list or library.

!

Important

SharePoint Designer update

As Microsoft suggested, InfoPath 2013 and SharePoint Designer 2013 will be the last versions of those products. SharePoint Designer is not being re-released with SharePoint Server 2016, although we will continue to support custom workflows built with SharePoint Designer and hosted on SharePoint Server 2016 and Office 365. Support for InfoPath 2013 and SharePoint Designer 2013 will match the support lifecycle for SharePoint Server 2016, running until 2026.

Reference:
https://blogs.office.com/2016/01/20/sharepoint-server-2016-and-project-server-2016-release-candidate-available/

Forms can be created for a number of data sources, including database connections, XML documents, and SharePoint lists and libraries. In this section, I'll be primarily focusing on default forms associated with a list and how you can create your own custom forms for the list or library using SharePoint Designer.

Note

Pre-requisite: SharePoint Designer 2013

SharePoint Designer 2013 is the tool of choice for the rapid development of SharePoint applications.

Download Link: https://www.microsoft.com/en-in/download/details.aspx?id=35491

First thing first...

1. Open SharePoint Designer 2013 (run as administrator)
2. Open your site in SharePoint Designer, click Lists and Libraries from Navigation pane.
3. Click the desired list from the gallery, for example, Announcements

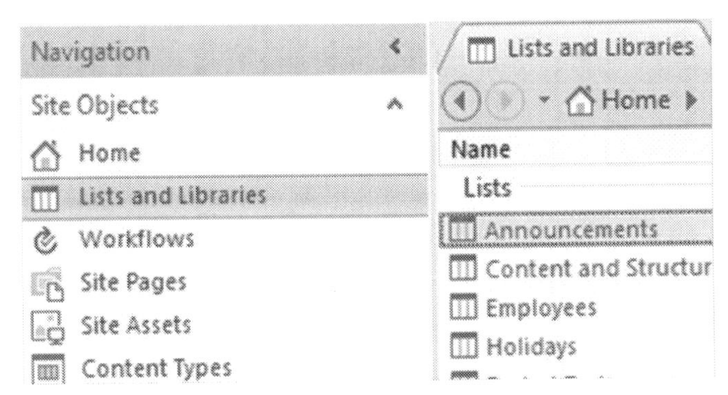

Figure 6.1 SharePoint Designer – Navigation Pane

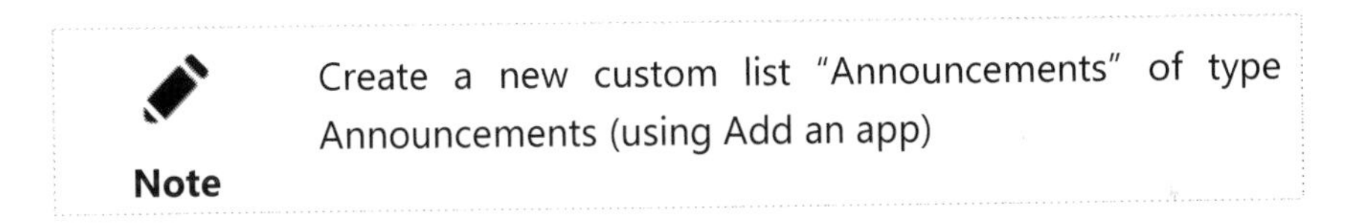

Note

Create a new custom list "Announcements" of type Announcements (using Add an app)

Figure 6.2 Announcements Template

4. On the summary page, you can see Announcements list details like views, forms, workflows, etc.

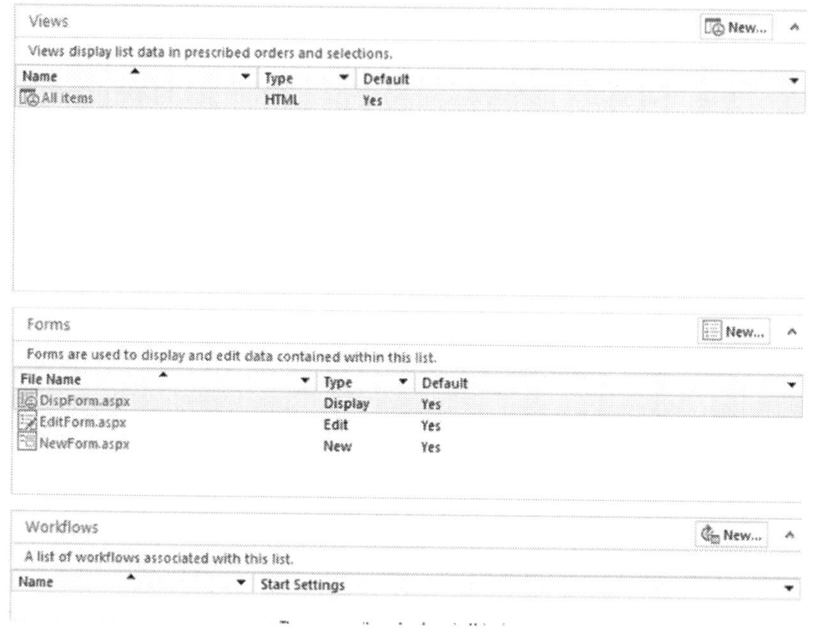

Figure 6.3 List Summary Page

5. Under Forms, click New button.

6. A new dialog box will open. Set the following properties to create a new form.

   a. File Name: NewItem.aspx (Make sure you type a unique name to avoid conflict with existing forms)

   b. Select the type of form to create: New item form (used to add new items to the list)

   c. Set as default form for the selected type: Check

Note

Once checked then this form will become the default form associated with our list. So next time onwards on any new item creation, this form will be displayed instead of original NewForm.aspx.

d. Click OK to save the form.

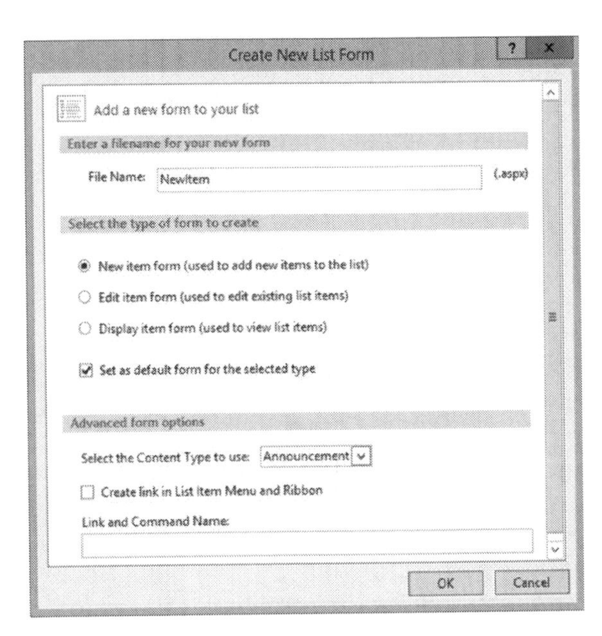

Figure 6.3 Create New List Form Options

You just created a new custom form called "NewItem.aspx". Open Announcements list in the browser and click new announcement. You can verify that our newly created form is displayed instead of original newForm.aspx.

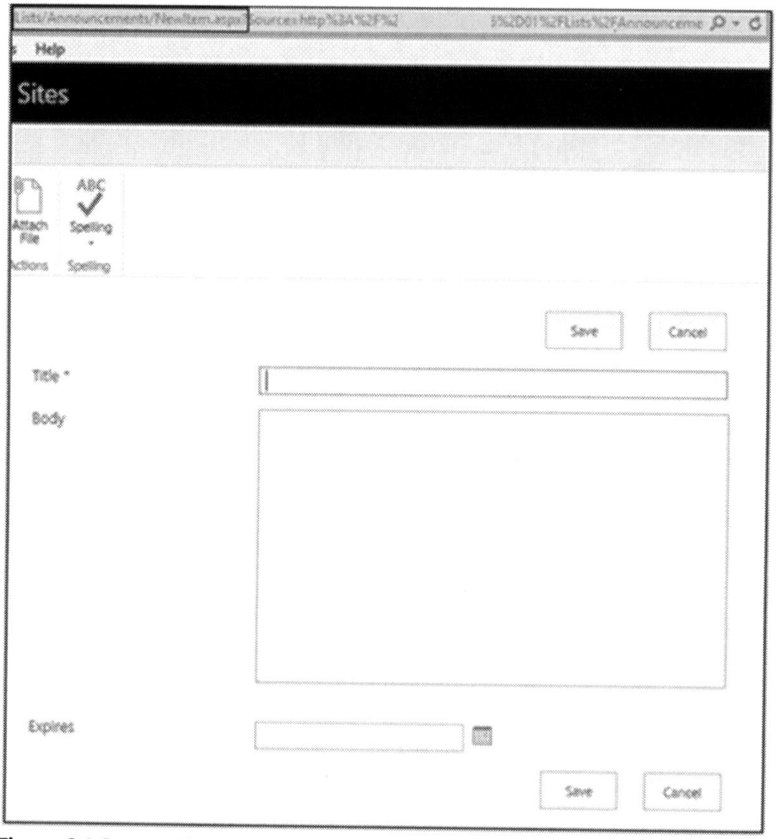

Figure 6.4 Custom List Form

Now, we will further customize this form to display controls in single column format. We will also hide top buttons (save and close). Let's switch back to SharePoint Designer again.

On Announcement Summary page, right-click on NewItem.aspx and click Edit File in advance mode.

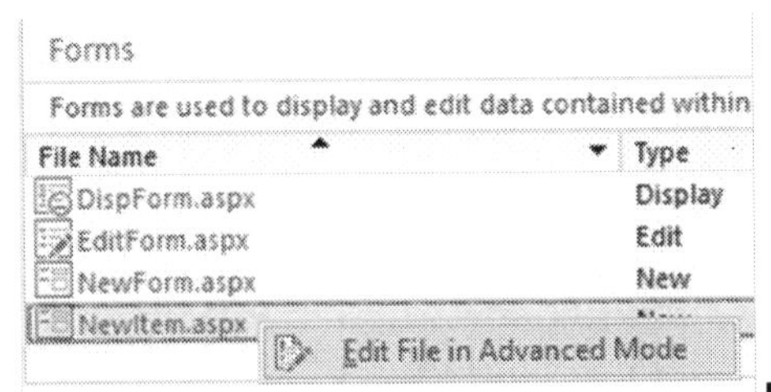

Figure 6.5 Edit File in Advanced Mode

This form will be opened in HTML editor in edit mode. Find id "savebutton1" and comment the entire table row using <!-- -->

```
<!--<tr>
    <td class="ms-toolbar" nowrap="nowrap">
        <table>
            <tr>
                <td width="99%" class="ms-toolbar" nowrap="nowrap"><IMG SRC="/_layouts/15/im
                <td class="ms-toolbar" nowrap="nowrap">
                    <SharePoint:SaveButton runat="server" ControlMode="New" id="savebutton1"
                </td>
                <td class="ms-separator"> </td>
                <td class="ms-toolbar" nowrap="nowrap" align="right">
                    <SharePoint:GoBackButton runat="server" ControlMode="New" id="gobackbutt
                </td>
            </tr>
        </table>
    </td>
</tr>-->
```

Figure 6.6 Comment HTML Elements

Save the form, by hitting Ctrl+S or save icon from the top menu. SPD will show a warning message box, click yes to continue.

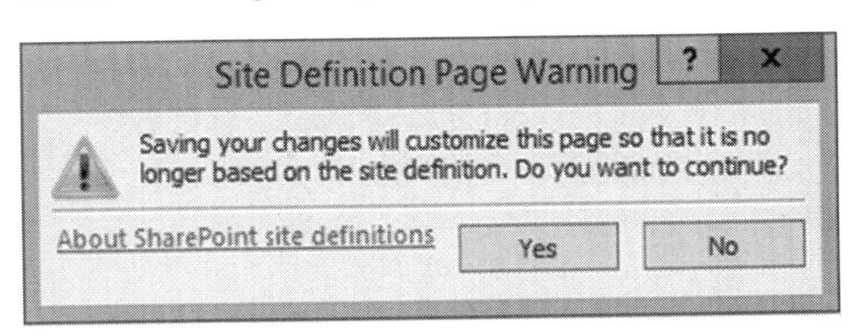

Figure 6.7 Site Definition Page Warning

Go back to browser and refresh NewItem.aspx form and those buttons are hidden now.

You need to format the table now, to display controls in a single row. Go back to SPD to modify the new form.

Find "Title" and you will realize that there are two sections (TDs) for displaying label and controls separately. All we need to do is to CUT input controls from 2nd TD and PASTE below label control in the first TD. To keep the same consistent look and feel, we will add these controls within a DIV element with the same class applied on TD.

Overall, it would look like below.

```
<tr>
    <td width="190px" valign="top" class="ms-formlabel">
        <H3 class="ms-standardheader">
            <nobr>Title<span class="ms-formvalidation"> *</span>
            </nobr>
        </H3>
        <div class="ms-formbody">
            <SharePoint:FormField runat="server" id="ff1{$Pos}" ControlMode="New" FieldName="Title" _
            <SharePoint:FieldDescription runat="server" id="ff1description{$Pos}" FieldName="Title" Co
        </div>
    </td>
</tr>
<tr>
    <td width="190px" valign="top" class="ms-formlabel">
        <H3 class="ms-standardheader">
            <nobr>Body</nobr>
        </H3>
        <div class="ms-formbody">
        <SharePoint:FormField runat="server" id="ff2{$Pos}" ControlMode="New" FieldName="Body" __desig
        <SharePoint:FieldDescription runat="server" id="ff2description{$Pos}" FieldName="Body" Control
        </div>
    </td>
</tr>
<tr>
    <td width="190px" valign="top" class="ms-formlabel">
        <H3 class="ms-standardheader">
            <nobr>Expires</nobr>
        </H3>
        <div class="ms-formbody">
        <SharePoint:FormField runat="server" id="ff3{$Pos}" ControlMode="New" FieldName="Expires" __de
        <SharePoint:FieldDescription runat="server" id="ff3description{$Pos}" FieldName="Expires" Cont
        </div>
```

Figure 6.8 Custom Form in HTML Mode

Save the changes to the form. Refresh your page in a browser to verify the changes.

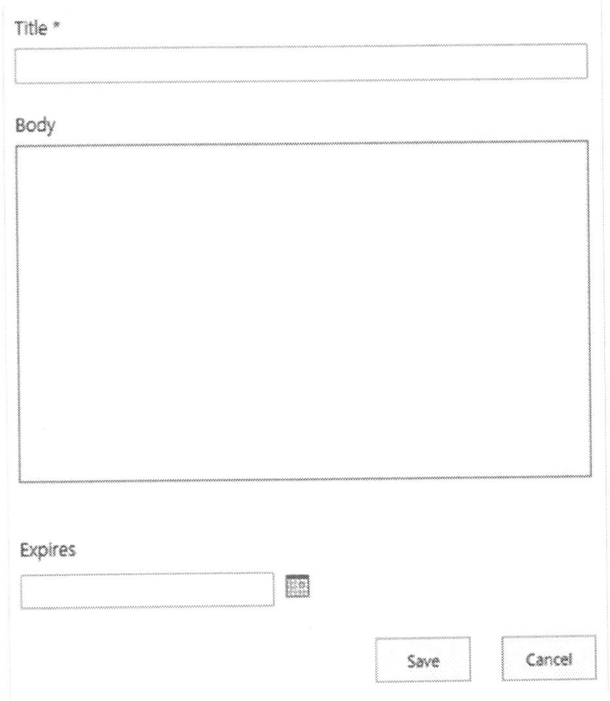

Title *

Body

Expires

Save Cancel

Figure 6.9 Custom Form Layout

How Wonderful!!! Next what? Just start customizing the form to suit your needs.....

SHAREPOINT DESIGNER WORKFLOWS

Each organization has various processes such as document approval, reimbursement request, etc. In simpler words, a workflow can be defined as the orchestrator of processes that allows you to model and automate business processes.

You can create workflows using SharePoint Designer (SPD) tool without any code or with very little customizations. SPD provides pre-loaded workflow templates to work with. There is three type of workflows that you can create using SPD. You can also think of it as scope for the workflow.

List: You can create and associate workflows to a single list or library within a SharePoint site. You need to create a separate workflow for each list / library.

Reusable: Unlike List Workflow, you can create Reusable Workflow, if you need to associate the same workflow to multiple lists or libraries. Reusable Workflow is primarily associated to Content Types. Once created, all lists or libraries inheriting that Content Type will initiate the workflow execution.

Site: Unlike List and Reusable workflow, site workflow is independent of all lists and libraries. Site Workflows are mainly used to achieve specific tasks which can look in every list within SharePoint site. For example, if you want to generate a report, to get the total count of users, then Site Workflow is a way to go.

Important

Workflow Manager for SharePoint 2016 (on-premises)

As we all know that with standard SharePoint installation, you will get only 2010 workflows options. In order to get the 2016 workflow engine, you need to configure the Workflow Manager. Even in 2016, it is still saying 2013 workflows (yes it is), because it is the same engine as we have seen in 2013

Reference:
http://social.technet.microsoft.com/wiki/contents/articles/34407.sharepoint-2016-step-by-step-installation-of-workflow-manager.aspx

Note

This is an advanced topic which requires technical expertise and hence out of the scope of this book

In this section, I'll walk you through to create a List Workflow on our previously created list Announcements. Using this List Workflow, we will send an email notification to users, once an item is added to Announcements list.

1. Open SharePoint Designer 2013 (run as administrator)
2. Open your site in SharePoint Designer, click Lists and Libraries in Navigation pane.
3. Click Announcements list.

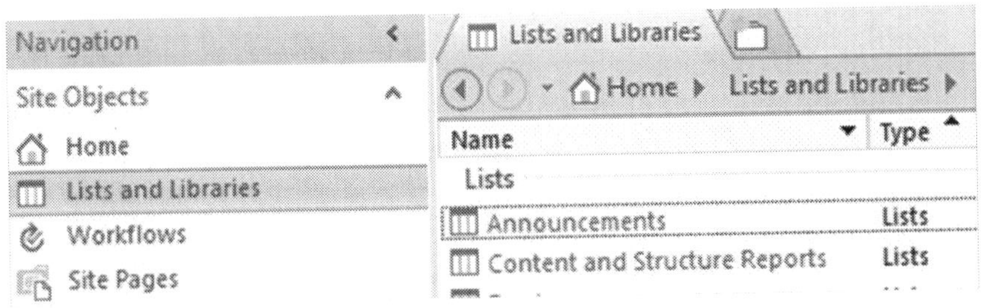

Figure 6.10 Navigation Pane in SharePoint Designer

4. Under Workflows section, click New

Figure 6.11 New Button to Create workflow

5. Set name to "Announcement Email"
6. Select "SharePoint 2010 Workflow" from Platform Type drop down list

Note

If workflow manager is not configured, you can use 2010 template as well.

7. Click OK

It will open a new editor.

8. Click Step1 header and set it to Step1: Send Email
9. Click on orange cursor
10. Click Action icon from the top menu. It will show you a drop down menu with various actions.
11. Click **Send an Email**

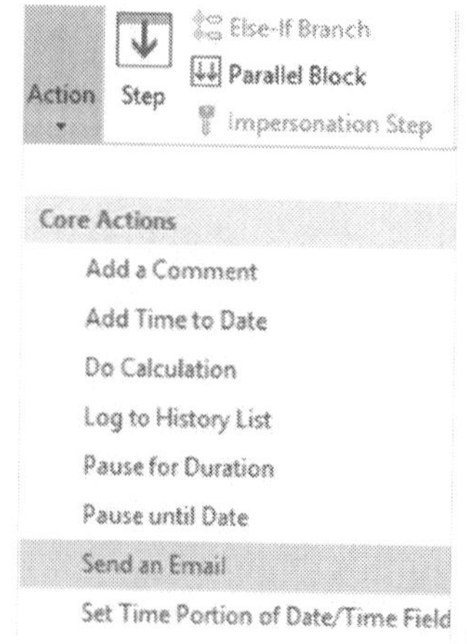

Figure 6.12 Add Action "Send an Email"

12. You can see that a new action has been added
13. Click Email **these users**
14. It will open a new dialog box to define a message

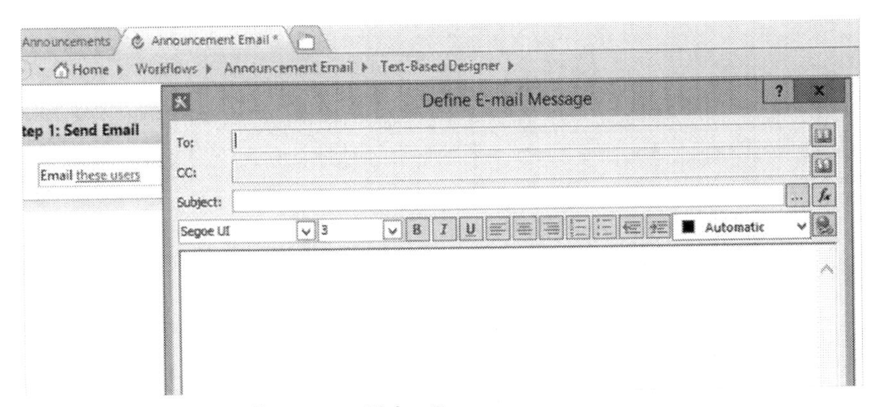

Figure 6.13 Define E-mail Message Dialog Box

15. Click Address book icon for To field
16. Type **everyone** in text box for Type a Name or E-mail Address and hit enter

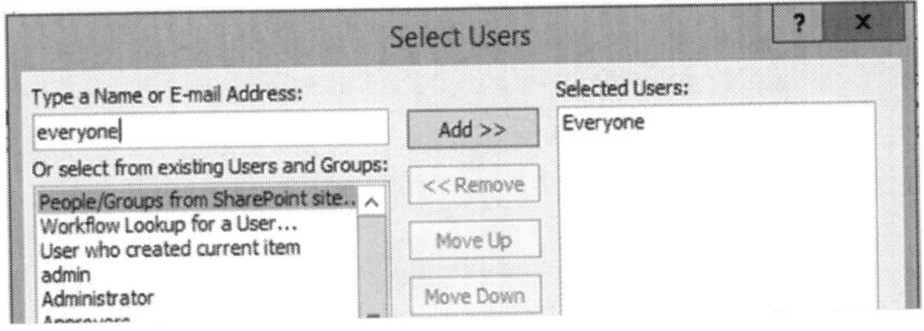

Figure 6.14 Setting Users to Send Mail

17. Click OK
18. Set Subject to **New Announcement!!!**
19. In body section, insert the following contents

Hi All,

A new announcement has been added.

Go to Announcement section at our Intranet Portal.

Best,
IT Team

20. Click OK

Your mail message will look like this.

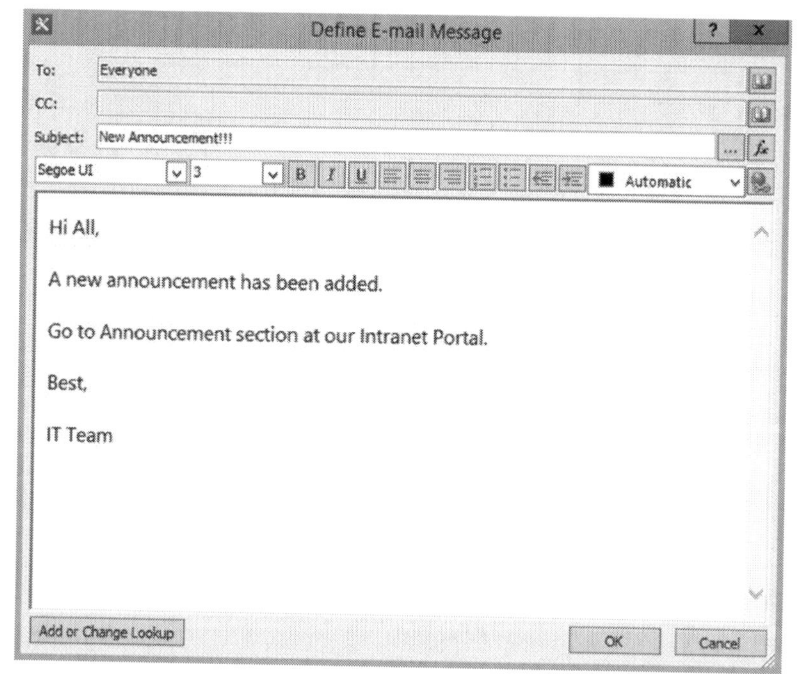

Figure 6.15 E-mail Message Defined

You have completed the action activity and proceed to set the workflow execution settings.

1. Click **Workflow Settings** from top ribbon

Figure 6.16 Workflow Settings

2. Under Start Options, unselect (clear checkbox) **Allow this workflow to be manually started**
3. Select (check) **Start workflow automatically when an item is created**
4. Unselect (clear check) **Start workflow automatically when an item is changed**
5. Click **Save** (it will take few minutes to save the workflow)
6. Click **Publish**

Figure 6.17 Save and Publish Icons

Hooray!!! You just create your first workflow.

You can also create a Reusable workflow or Site workflow using the same procedure with the following modification. Instead of selecting the List Workflow button, in the ribbon select the **Reusable Workflow** or **Site Workflow** button when creating the workflow.

Summary:

This chapter provided you a high-level knowledge about creating custom forms and its capabilities. You should also understand the working of workflows that can be associated with a list or library.

Develop It Yourself – Exercises 6.0

Scenario: Your manager wants to receive an email notification each time a new product document is added. You need to create a new workflow to send a notification with small product information within the mail.

1. Create a new workflow
2. Set workflow settings to run on item creation
3. Define mail template to include product information in subject and body of the mail.
   a. Subject – Product Title
   b. Body – Author and Keywords

To get step-by-step instructions of exercises 6.0, visit our site.

DIY

FAREWELL

At the end of this journey, we covered "What and How" of SharePoint 2016 out-of-the-box web parts and features in action. This should provide you a head start to plan and deliver quick wins at your workplace.

Personally, I do not consider it as a farewell but a new opportunity for you to start a new journey to become a SharePoint Expert, eventually...

REFERENCES

Writing technical book requires a lot of efforts in understanding core topics and creating working samples. I used these Microsoft sites as a reference which really guided me to get insights about Microsoft SharePoint 2016 definitions using technical blogs, articles, and examples.

https://technet.microsoft.com/en-us/

https://support.office.com/

WHAT DO YOU THINK OF THIS BOOK?

We want to hear from you! Participate at our website.

icodie.com

Tell us how well this book meets your needs—what works effectively, and what we can do better. Your feedback will help us continually improve our books and learning resources for you.

info@icodie.com

Thank you in advance for your input!

Made in the USA
San Bernardino, CA
01 January 2018